The Magic of
Birds

The Magic of
Birds

Celia Fisher

THE BRITISH LIBRARY

First published in 2014 by
The British Library
96 Euston Road
London NW1 2DB

British Library Cataloguing-in-Publication Data
A catalogue record for this publication is available from the British Library

ISBN 978 0 7123 5742 5

Designed and typeset by Andrew Shoolbred
Printed in Hong Kong by Great Wall Printing Co. Ltd

CONTENTS

CHAPTER ONE

Creation and Diversity

Various creation myths have involved birds. In ancient Egypt the *benu* bird flew over the primordial flood waters, and from its call existence began. Presumably it was also responsible for the cosmic egg, laid in the mud as the flood receded, from which the sun god Ra emerged. The bird and the god shared the attributes of daily rebirth. Over time this mythological Egyptian bird took various forms, including a yellow wagtail and a hieroglyphic heron. By classical times it lost its watery associations and became a fiery eagle and finally a phoenix. Meanwhile the idea of the cosmic egg grew larger until it could only have been laid by an ostrich. Far to the north, the Finnish creation myth, as recorded in the nineteenth-century epic poem the *Kalevala*, set the watery scene in a dark and endless ocean with a sacred duck flying over in search of a resting place. The goddess of air and water, taking pity on its plight, raised her knees out of the icy water and there it laid its egg. But, as her lap grew uncomfortably warm, the goddess shook herself and the eggshell cracked apart, turning into the sky and the earth and, in the traditional storyteller's chant, 'from the yolk the sun was made, from the white the moon was formed'. The biblical Book of Genesis also began with darkness on the face of the deep, but no egg. God acted as the prime mover and it was not until the fifth day – after dividing light from darkness, earth from sea, and setting over them the sun, moon and stars – that God said, 'let the waters bring forth abundantly the moving creature that hath life, and fowl that may fly above the earth in the open firmament of heaven'. Those early attempts at physics and biology may now seem overly poetic, but the wonder inspired by the mystery of life's forms – including creatures that could fly and sing, lay eggs and sprout many-coloured feathers – marked the origins of scientific inquiry.

The diversity of birds is part of the message that the medieval manuscript illuminator sought to convey. By the fourteenth century a fascination with the real world caused religious manuscripts (and church carvings) to be decorated with natural details, including foliage and birds, which were often excitingly accurate. Picture Bibles, of which this is an example produced in London around 1330, retold the Christian story through selected highlights using large pictures and small captions (the medieval equivalent of cartoons). A Dominican friar appeared on the opening page instructing the artist to make his pictures clear, for they were the means to teach the Word; and for the illustration of God creating the birds the illuminator evidently felt that a wide range of birds was needed to do justice to God's powers. Above God's left shoulder perch a goldfinch, magpie, sparrow and robin. Beside his right hand sit a horned owl and a bullfinch, and over his head a fieldfare and red-beaked chough. Above them on either side are the more exotic birds, a peacock to the left and on the right a blue bird flying much like a crane. Between them fly a thrush, a chaffinch, a swallow and a kite. On the far right a pelican is improbably perched on a fig tree feeding its young from its own blood – not that pelicans do any such thing, but the manner in which they regurgitate food from their huge beaks into the mouths of nestlings was misrepresented and misinterpreted, causing them to become widespread emblems of Christ's sacrifice.

It is especially remarkable with the birds depicted in flight that the fourteenth-century artist has attempted to capture their 'jizz'. Jizz is a word of uncertain origin, probably derived from 'guise' meaning appearance (now obsolete and defined by its opposite, disguise), although it may have a much more recent derivation from an abbreviation of 'general impression of size and shape', an Air Force expression used for recognising enemy aircraft. Either way, jizz is the word used by birdwatchers to describe the particular features of birds, and it often relies on the unique way in which a species hops, wades, perches or flies, because with creatures so characterised by movement jizz

OPPOSITE: God creating the birds from the Holkham Bible, 14th century.

Oment deu li puyssaunt. En le syr fesoyt oysel volaunt. Arbres diuerses
serryt portaunt. Jeceus q' estoyent auenaunz. De tere synt cretie erbes z flu
res. De queus les miures sount lurs cures. Bestes sure tere: en elwe peyson
ke ren ne esest saunluy noun. Car p'luy tut eset. Ceel z tere z taunt q' est.
Cum yle pensoyt z le uouspt. Been tot su feet ceo dyt le seryt. Ken ne syst de
sa mesin. Stors home z femme ceo sorez certeyn. Tutes choses syl fesoyt slurisse
z tut yle fesoyt pur homme seruyr.

makes for easier identification than details of shape or colour. Naturally the way a forked-tailed swallow swoops on the air is quite different from the glide of a bird of prey, or the heavy flapping of a crane, or the brisk wing-beats of a small bird, and something of this has been caught on the stillness of the page. So too has the characteristic balance of the perching peacock, owl and magpie. But jizz is not entirely about movement. The feature that identifies the chough is its red beak and legs, otherwise it would look much like any other black member of the crow family. This chough may be a further example of the artist's wish to include unusual birds, because its habitat is confined to coastal cliffs. Since most clues suggest that this manuscript was produced in London it is doubly intriguing that the medieval artist knew what a chough looked like.

At the end of the same century, around 1400, an artist called John Siferwas was commissioned by the Abbey of Sherborne to decorate a sumptuous missal (designed for priests to read the different Masses throughout the year). Birds did not appear in prayer books as part of the narrative, as they might in a Bible, but it was not unusual by this date for them to feature in the decorative margins. The trend seems to have started in Italy, as part of the early Renaissance movement towards realism, and spread northwards. But no manuscript in Europe contains as many different species of birds as the *Sherborne Missal*. It includes a total of over fifty (both male and female in some cases), many identified by evocative old English names – sparwe, throstil, ruddock and titmose – and nearly all recognisable, although with varying degrees of jizz. The woodpecker and kingfisher are there and, though their vivid colours have faded over time, the kingfisher looks poised to dart for a fish and the woodpecker's long tongue coils from its mouth as it raises

Woodpecker from the *Sherborne Missal*, c.1399–1407.

Fieldfare from the *Sherborne Missal*, c.1399–1407.

its head to tap for insects and suck them up. There are fat quails and woodcocks, pheasants, geese and ducks, such as the monks might relish eating, but no birds of prey. And there are no members of the crow family except for a jay. The seabirds include a cormorant with characteristically huge feet, a gannet, a seagull and a bar-tailed godwit – and the latter demonstrated the artist's exceptional aptitude for depicting brown birds, dispelling any sense of dullness in the colour by delighting in the intricate patterns of their feathers. Another example of this is the fierce-looking fieldfare, sitting on a curving branch of red berries, a decorative device but also a reminder of the hawthorn berries that fieldfares flock for in autumn.

An equally fierce shrike has its breast feathers tinted with pink. This is strange because the pink colouring is typical of the lesser grey shrike native to southern Europe, rather than the great grey shrike of northern Europe. It raises the possibility that the Italian influence stimulating the illuminators of Europe included the circulation of pattern books containing bird studies. Few have survived (although they were precious at the time, they were subjected to repeated copying and then probably fell to pieces or went out of fashion) but their existence is further proof that in the fourteenth century some artists sketched from nature. The most remarkable remaining model book is indeed Italian, created by Giovannino de' Grassi (d. 1398). He was the principal architect of Milan Cathedral as well as a leading manuscript illuminator commanding a large workshop. His model book, which would have been used by his apprentices, included a decorated Gothic alphabet and exquisite animal and bird studies. One English pattern book also survives, with four pages of bird drawings. It dates from about 1400, and

Shrike from the *Sherborne Missal*,
c.1399–1407.

in the seventeenth century came into the library of Samuel Pepys. Given this evidence it seems likely that the birds in the *Sherborne Missal* were selected from a similar sketchbook, which must have included precious studies of unusual birds. And the existence of such model books, changing hands and being in turn copied, might also help to explain how the coastal chough appeared in the Picture Bible produced in London.

Was it due to the varying quality of available models that the rarer birds in the *Sherborne Missal* tended to be better represented? Not always – the robin, wren and sparrows are full of character. It is mainly the tits and finches in the missal that are too elongated and poorly coloured to do justice to these pretty, rounded little birds, with the one exception of the rarer long-tailed tit. A better example of a blue tit, excellent both for colouring and jizz, precedes all these, having hopped into the border of a biblical history of the world dated around 1290. All these are signs that the variety of bird species could be appreciated as keenly in the past as now, but no particular rationale was sought to explain this diversity, except in terms of God's creative skills. So while differences of appearance and behaviour could be observed, they were not examined. Take the feeding habits of tits. Since they all forage for caterpillars, insects and spiders competition needs to be reduced by adaptation to different trees. The coal tit, which is the smallest and most agile, seeks out conifers where it can insert its tiny beak between the needles. The great tit, being the largest species, settles for the lower part of any tree and the inner branches where it can forage and nest more freely, leaving the higher and outer parts of trees to the somewhat smaller blue tit, which is nimble enough to hang on to thin twigs, looking for food in tighter places and nesting in smaller holes. On the other hand fierce competition exists within a species when it comes to mating. The dancing, fluttering displays of feathers and the intricacies of birdsong are designed for this purpose, and as well as fine plumage it seems that the male bird with the best repertoire of minute variations in his theme tune is sexier and more likely to get the female and the territory of his choice.

Blue tit from the *Historia scholastica*,
late 13th century

The dawning fascination in Europe with indigenous birds, their similarities and differences, was augmented by accounts of the discovery of new lands and strange fowl. Marco Polo, arriving in southwest India on his way home to Europe from China, wrote, 'there are parrots of many sorts, some white as snow with red beaks and feet, some red or blue or green, forming the most charming sight in the world. They have also very beautiful peacocks and cocks and hens quite different from ours.' The Portuguese explorer Ferdinand Magellan, on going through the straits that led him to the Pacific, encountered penguins in huge quantities and described them as ducks without wings or, on closer inspection, black geese with all their feathers alike, both on body and wings, and a beak like a crow. In the sixteenth century came fabulous accounts of birds of paradise found on the Indonesian islands. Another Portuguese explorer, Luis Vaz de Camoens, substantiated the myth of 'golden birds which have no feet and never descend to the ground'; and the sixteenth-century Spanish explorer José de Acosta: 'their whole bodies are feathers and they hang upon boughs by strings or feathers and so rest themselves like airy things'. During the sixteenth century such exotic birds appeared on maps as markers of the continents (penguins not until 1608). Africa was traditionally the land of the ostrich, parrot and sometimes secretary bird. Spread across the Orient were pheasants, cranes and the occasional bird of paradise or hornbill (starting with Le Testu's world map of 1566; see below). As for the New World, in 1550 Pierre Desceliers, who belonged to the Dieppe school of cartography, produced a map depicting a turkey for the first time and from then on these birds typified North America; as a later map-maker explained, 'this country abounds chiefly in turkies whose plenty deserves no less admiration than their bulk'. In South America Desceliers placed a macaw, and in 1593 a map of Brazil and Peru in Cornelis de Jode's *Speculum Orbis Terrae* showed a toucan and a rhea.

The most colourful map-maker of the sixteenth century was Guillaume Le Testu, who ended his life in 1573 as a buccaneer fighting alongside Francis Drake against

ABOVE: Turkey from the Desceliers World Map, by Pierre Desceliers, 1550.

OPPOSITE: Flamingo, drawing by John White, 1585–93. British Museum.

the Spaniards at Nombre de Dios. Le Testu, like Desceliers, was a Dieppe cartographer, who in 1552 had been sent by Henri II to chart the South American coast. In 1555 he was involved alongside Admiral Coligny in trying to found a French colony near Rio de Janeiro. On his return to France he published a world atlas of fifty-six pages (in 1556, reissued in 1566), dedicated to Coligny. Le Testu's maps included signature birds marking different parts of the world, including the first bird of paradise. Most arresting of all was the distant landmass of Great Java or Terra Australis, the unknown continent where, Le Testu admitted, 'there has never yet been any man who has made a certain discovery of it'. Le Testu advocated approaching what later proved to be Australia through the Straits of Magellan, and there he placed what appear to be black swans and cassowaries.

Did Le Testu, during their historic encounter, help to inspire Drake's circumnavigation of 1576–8? The two privateers had much in common, including draughtsmanship. A Portuguese pilot described Drake spending long hours aboard the *Golden Hind* locked in his cabin with an assistant, making drawings: 'he kept a book in which he entered his navigation and in which he delineated birds, trees and sea lions. He is adept at painting and has with him a boy, a relative of his, who is a great painter. When they both shut themselves up in his cabin they were always painting.' There is a surviving French album, *Histoire Naturelle des Indes*, with primitive illustrations linked to Drake's voyages. Such 'paper museums' were more transportable and useful for reference than dead specimens, and in 1584 Richard Hakluyt went on record proposing that 'a skilful painter is also to be carried with you, which the Spaniards used commonly in all their discoveries, to bring the descriptions of all beasts, birds, fishes, towns etc'. This was the task of John White, gentleman artist, when he sailed with Richard Grenville's expedition to Virginia (now North Carolina) in 1585. On Roanoke Island he made many watercolours of the Algonquin Indians, but the surviving bird studies by White's own hand seem to have been made when the ships were making their way through the West Indies. His frigate bird, tropic bird, booby and tern

A Flaminco.

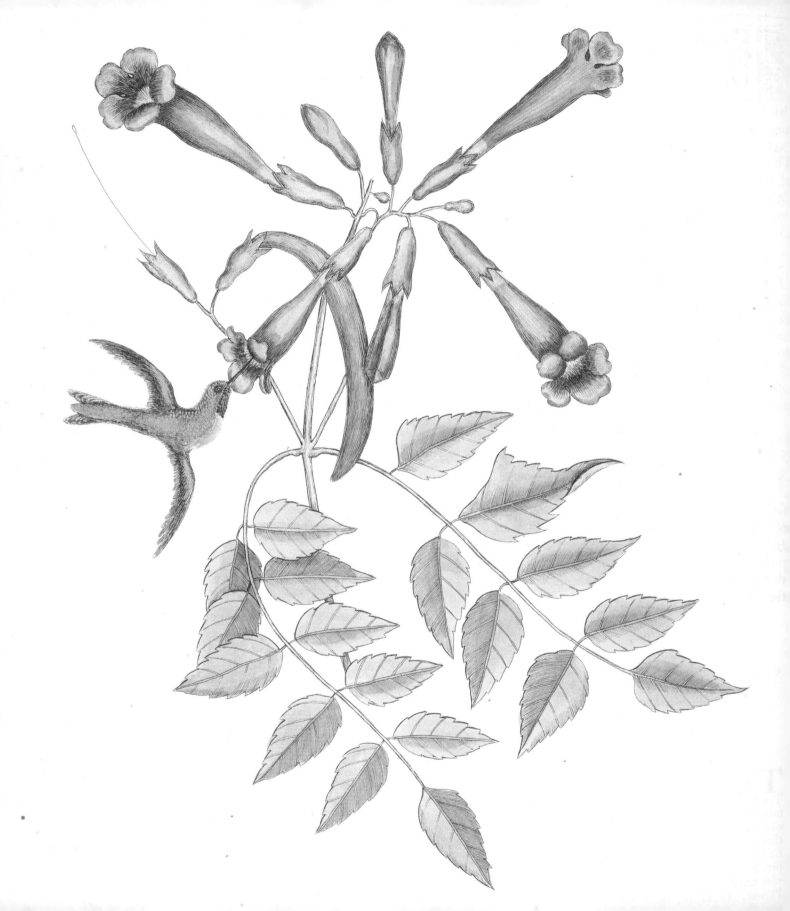

(or noddy) are all tropical seabirds and good to eat – thus fulfilling the utilitarian remit of White's artistic employment. But his exquisite watercolour of a flamingo, capturing the extraordinary proportions of its legs and beak (designed to filter food from mud) and the softness of its pink feathers (the pigment varying with the bird's diet) is surely, even though flamingos are edible, a celebration of the enticing beauty to be found in the lagoons of this brave New World. John White continued to paint birds when he reached North Carolina. His fellow scientist Thomas Harriot, in his *Brief and True Report*, mentions a set depicting '8 water and 17 land fowl although we have seen and eaten many more'. There are twenty-seven surviving watercolours of birds, mostly inscribed with Algonquian names, which may be copies of White's lost originals. This collection, some more naive than others, includes a bald eagle, sandhill crane, great northern diver and golden oriole, a woodpecker (but perched like a pigeon) and a blue jay (but credited with the mimicking skills of a mockingbird). By far the most striking of the set is the northern cardinal bird, so vivid and red that even a sixteenth-century Protestant might have acknowledged the name. It is gifted with a repertoire of tuneful whistling songs almost as irresistible as its appearance.

From then on the birds of the New World exerted a strong fascination, whether they were colourful variations on a familiar theme such as wrens, tits, finches and swallows, or entirely exotic like hummingbirds. Works were published by observers in the field such as Mark Catesby who, on returning to England, brought out his *Natural History of Carolina* in 1754, with alluring descriptions of bird behaviour: 'the Carolina humming bird with a body the size of a humble bee, and its tongue a tube through which it sucks honey'. The birds 'rove from flower to flower on which they wholly subsist and sometimes by thrusting too far into the flower they get caught'. Other eighteenth-century publications included the wonderfully eclectic *Natural History of Uncommon Birds*, compiled by George Edwards, librarian to the Royal College of Physicians. He illustrated birds live or stuffed as they came into the collections of naturalists such as

ABOVE: Red cardinal, drawing by John White, 1585-93.

OPPOSITE: Hummingbird from *The Natural History of Carolina, Florida and the Bahama Islands,* by Mark Catesby, 1748.

ABOVE: Horned owl from
A Natural History of Uncommon Birds,
by George Edwards, 1743–51.

OPPOSITE: Toucan from
A Natural History of Uncommon Birds,
by George Edwards, 1743–51.

Hans Sloane, or aristocrats such as Lord Burlington, to whom he owed his image of a great horned owl: 'I saw this bird alive in the park of his lordship's house at Chiswick. It was brought from Virginia. There is now kept alive at the Mourning Bush Tavern by Aldersgate an owl which I take to be the same species.' The very appealing toucan depicted by George Edwards was also a live specimen, brought back by 'the King's Attorney General for the Island of Jamaica'.

However, it was John James Audubon, in *The Birds of America*, published between 1827 and 1839, who really conveyed the range of feathered creatures inhabiting North America. Audubon was born on a sugar plantation in Haiti, the illegitimate son of a French naval officer with freebooting ways, who reared him in France during the Revolution but (to escape Napoleon's conscription) then set up his son in business and property in America. Unlikely as it sounds, his father also endowed Audubon with a passion for birds: 'he would point out the elegant movement of birds, the beauty and softness of their plumage. He called my attention to their show of pleasure or sense of danger, their perfect forms and splendid attire. He would speak of their departure and return with the seasons.' For Audubon success came after a long struggle, dogged by bankruptcy and the destruction of many paintings (and birds). Finally, having been rebuffed for publication in America, he achieved recognition during his visit to England and Scotland in 1826. There followed sponsorship and the publication of his aptly named double-elephant folios, a total of 435 enormous colour plates in four volumes together with five separate volumes of *Ornithological Biographies*, the latter proving how minutely he observed bird behaviour as well as appearance. For instance, one of his most famous plates is the wild turkey, but his description of their group migrations in search of food is almost better:

> If their progress (on foot) is interrupted by a river they betake themselves to the highest eminence and often remain a whole day as if for the purpose of consultation. The males are heard gobbling, making much ado and strutting about as if to raise their courage

The Bill Bird   by George Edwards 1745

Pica Brasiliensis. Toucan

64   Ramphastos - piscivorus.

Wild turkey from *The Birds of America*,
by John James Audubon, 1827–38.

to a pitch. Even the females and young spread their tails, run round each other and perform extravagant leaps. When the weather is settled and all is quiet they all mount to the tops of the highest trees, and at a signal consisting of a single cluck given by a leader, the flock takes flight to the opposite shore. The old fat birds easily get over but the younger frequently fall in the water. They then bring their wings close to their body, spread out their tail as a support, stretch forward their neck and striking out their legs with great vigour proceed rapidly to the shore. If they find it too steep for landing they float downstream till they come to an accessible part and by a violent effort generally extricate themselves from the water. But immediately after thus crossing a large river they ramble about for some time as if bewildered.

Less affectionately absurd, indeed full of Victorian sentiment, is Audubon's description of the courtship rituals of a mockingbird:

See how he flies round his mate with motions as light as a butterfly. His tail is widely expanded, he mounts in the air to a small distance, describes a circle and again alighting approaches his beloved one, his eyes gleaming with delight. His beautiful wings are gently raised, he bows to his love, and again bouncing upwards opens his bill and pours forth his melody, full of exultation at the conquest he has made.

Mockingbirds inspire great affection. Even in America, with its gun culture, hunters have proved unwilling to shoot them. This is partly on account of their endearing habit of nesting as near human habitation as possible – 'so well', as Audubon put it, 'does the bird know that man is not his most dangerous enemy' – and also for the marvel of their singing repertoire. 'The mellowness of the song, the varied modulations and gradations, the great brilliancy of execution are unrivalled.' As well as beauty there is amusement because

a mockingbird, as its name implies, relishes imitating the sounds of other birds, 'plunging from the shrill kee kee of the sunflower bird to the irascible qua-ack of a blue jay, to the sad lament of poor will, poor will, poor will' – thus Harper Lee in *To Kill a Mockingbird*, using the bird as a leitmotif in her novel of racial tensions in twentieth-century America. The vulnerability of this harmless, appealing songster struck Audubon too. Instead of illustrating its joyous courtship dance he chose to show its nest under hideous attack from a coiled snake.

During his promotional tour of 1826 Audubon went to Edinburgh and found the beauty of the city equalled by the warmth of his welcome, his only regret being that Sir Walter Scott never came to any of his presentations. However the young Charles Darwin, then a medical student at Edinburgh University, did attend a demonstration that Audubon gave on his method of propping dead birds into life-like positions with wire. A decade later Darwin, on the voyage of HMS *Beagle*, also turned his attention to mockingbirds. He was primarily interested in the links between species on islands and neighbouring continents, and in the Galapagos Islands he realised that the mockingbirds varied from one island to another, and that those he saw on Chatham and James Island resembled those he had seen in Chile, while on Charles Island and Albemarle they were different (and since none of these was a mimic they lacked the feature which had earned the North American mockingbird its name). In his notes on mockingbirds Darwin mused for the first recorded time about 'the stability of species', moving away from the orthodox creation theory towards the concept of a common ancestor from which variations evolved.

However, it was Darwin's finches that made the newspapers. In 1837 he showed those he had collected on the return voyage of the *Beagle* to John Gould, the great Victorian ornithologist, who declared them 'a series of ground finches which are so peculiar as to form an entirely new group'. (In fact there are up to fifteen different species and they are possibly closer to sparrows.) Their variations are not remarkable except for the size and shape of their beaks, ranging with subtle gradations from pointed to parrot-like, and highly adapted to different food sources. For instance, among the cactus-feeders, those with more pointed beaks can punch holes in the fruit of prickly pears to eat the pulp around the seeds, while those with shorter, thicker beaks tear at the cactus base for pulp and insects. Both eat the buds and flowers. When Darwin published *The Voyage of the Beagle* he touched on the theory of natural selection in describing his finches: 'seeing this gradation and diversity of structure in one small related group of birds, one might fancy that from an original paucity of birds in this archipelago one species has been taken and modified to different ends'. In *On the Origin of Species by Means of Natural Selection*, published in 1859, Darwin extended the question: 'the most striking and important fact is their affinity to those of the nearest mainland'. In the Galapagos almost all life forms have characteristics linked to the American mainland, and yet in geology, climate and size the islands are more like the Cape Verde archipelago, where the links are clearly to Africa. This could be explained not by the conventional view of divine creation but by the concept of species colonising, 'and that such colonists would be subject to modification ... the principal of inheritance still betraying their original birthplace'.

On the other side of the world, in the East Indies, Alfred Wallace had reached the same conclusion. It was the sheer abundance of species that puzzled Wallace and inspired him to become a naturalist. He regarded the emerging theory of evolution (at that stage called the 'transmutation of species') as 'an incitement to the collection of facts and an object to which they can be applied when collected'. Between 1854 and 1862, while in his thirties, he travelled through Malaysia and Indonesia and sent research papers back to the scientific community (including Darwin). In 1855 the conclusion to his latest paper became known as the Sarawak Law: 'every species has come into existence coincident both in space and time with a closely allied species'. Travelling eastwards Wallace identified a dividing line between creatures inhabiting the islands from Borneo and Bali westwards,

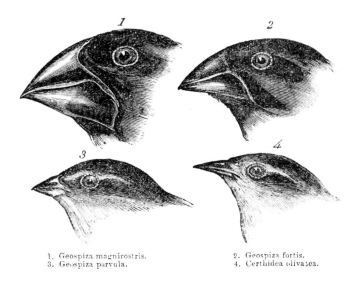

1. Geospiza magnirostris.
3. Geospiza parvula.

2. Geospiza fortis.
4. Certhidea olivasea.

ABOVE: Galapagos finches from *Journal of researches into the natural history and geology of the countries visited during the voyage of H.M.S. Beagle round the world, under the command of Capt. FitzRoy, R.N.*, by Charles Darwin, 1860.

OPPOSITE: *Paradisea minor* from *A Monograph of the Paradiseidæ; or, Birds of Paradise*, by Daniel Giraud Elliot, London, 1783.

J. Smit. lith.

M & N Hanhart imp

PARADISEA MINOR

which were related to Asia, and those to the east – Lombok, Sulawesi and New Guinea – which were related to Australia. The division was caused by the deep waters and currents of the Lombok Straits, which prevented colonisation, and it was named in his honour the Wallace Line. Eastwards were cockatoos and the fabled birds of paradise, and these discoveries caused Wallace to send another article in 1858 outlining the theory of natural selection and survival of the fittest, which Darwin had been working on for years but not yet published. Their papers were read together to the Linnean Society without causing any great sensation – but in 1859 Darwin published *On the Origin of Species by Means of Natural Selection* and the effect was momentous.

Meanwhile Wallace continued his travels in the East Indies, funding himself by hunting and collecting on a commercial scale. Sending home exotic birds was the way he earned his keep (though tenuously, because his journals would relate how he had to 'make a small parakeet do for two meals'). Birds of paradise had been hunted and traded long before Europeans arrived in the East. They had been so named (by those who saw them in Oriental markets as legless bundles of fabulous feathers) 300 years before Alfred Wallace tracked them in earnest from island to island. In 1869 he published vivid traveller's tales in *The Malay Archipelago* (the novelist Joseph Conrad's favourite book). The traditional method of trapping was by cords tightened around the birds' legs as they landed to feed on a favourite fruit tree or giant arum, after which they were tied to a perch, and their violent attempts to escape led to their legendary absence of legs. Wallace was the first to send specimens back to Europe in an unmutilated state, and when he himself returned in 1862 he brought with him two *Paradisaea minor* he had acquired in a Singapore market, which had most unusually survived being caged. Their diet was rice, bananas and cockroaches and Wallace spent his time in every port replenishing supplies (in a bakehouse in Malta he gratefully filled several biscuit tins with cockroaches). Arriving in Marseilles in March Wallace started to worry about frosts, but the birds were survivors, and finally reached Regent's Park Zoo, where

they were happy to display their plumage and would eat mealworms from the hands of admirers.

But nothing could equal the wild display of a whole tree full of birds of paradise preparing to mate. The American zoologist Daniel Giraud Elliot's *Monograph of the Paradiseidae*, published in 1873 with magnificent illustrations, was dedicated to Alfred Wallace and used his descriptions. For instance, he depicted the great bird of paradise, up to twenty of them in a tree:

> raising their wings, stretching their necks downwards and elevating their exquisite plumes into golden fans kept in continual vibration ... their loud shrill cries were the most prominent sound of the Aru Islands as they flew from branch to branch in great excitement, so that the whole tree was filled with waving plumes in every variety of attitude and motion.

Later Wallace was possibly even more enchanted by the king bird of paradise, writing 'how few Europeans had ever beheld the perfect little organisms I now gazed upon – the two middle feathers of the tail are in the form of slender wires which diverge into a beautiful curve, coloured a fine metallic green and curled spirally inward till they form a pair of elegant glittering buttons' and 'when the wings are elevated a band of emerald green feathers spread into a pair of elegant fans'. Perhaps at such a moment Wallace felt that the birds themselves outshone all scientific theories.

OPPOSITE: *Cicinnurus regius*, king bird of paradise, from *A Monograph of the Paradiseidae; or, Birds of Paradise*, by Daniel Giraud Elliot, London, 1873.

CHAPTER TWO

Oriental Birds

Much spiritual and philosophical teaching in Eastern tradition was done through exemplary tales in which birds and animals stood for human characteristics, provoking and resolving moral dilemmas. The origins of these fables were as old as storytelling and they were transmitted orally long before written versions were preserved in Indian literature. The Buddhist *Jataka Tales* date from around 400 BC and spread with Buddha's religious teaching to China, Japan and South East Asia. The Sanskrit version of around 200 BC, known as *Panchatantra* or Five Principles, filtered into Hindu literature and later inspired many Islamic texts under the new guise of the *Fables of Pilpay* or the *Kalila and Dimna Tales* (named after the two jackals who began the sequence). These were collected into luxuriously illustrated manuscripts for the delight of Indian, Persian and Turkish princes.

The story of the crows and owls, who hated one another, appears in the section of the *Panchatantra* (and all subsequent versions) called 'War and Peace'. It demonstrates the kinds of conflicts that arise from contrary natures and attitudes and the resolutions are positively Machiavellian (to use a European analogy), although they still resonate today since bird (like human) nature does not change. The precept, in the context of warfare, was that outwitting the enemy counts for more than brute force. The original authorship was attributed to Vishnu Sharma, a venerable sage who undertook to awaken intelligence in the king's three unteachable sons and make them masters of statecraft. The story began when the birds assembled to choose a king and every species put forward suggestions: the courageous falcon; the majestic eagle; the resplendent peacock (carrying a train of starry eyes on his tail). In the end several chose the owl because it was considered wise, but many others declared they would never obey so deformed a creature. The assembly broke up with bitter argument until a crow arrived on the scene (as they do when there is fighting) and was invited to mediate. The dramatic moment is illustrated here, when all the various birds are poised, or flying in, to hear the words of the crow. But the crow asked how on earth could they choose so ugly, despicable and malign a bird: 'are you such fools as to elect an owl that draws after him nothing but misfortune? – far better to live without a king'. In some versions the crow made a strong bid to become king himself. Meanwhile the owl flew off, full of resentment, and nothing would do for the crows but to seek to destroy the owls – which they achieved by first sending a crow to pose as a pathetic outcast. The owls were deceived and took him in, enabling him to learn their secrets, including the location of the cave where the owls assembled together. The crows then set the entrance to the cave alight, burning, suffocating and destroying all the owls gathered inside.

Some bird fables showed a far nobler spirit, for instance the pelican, which, during a season of drought when the birds were perishing from hunger and thirst, dispensed food and water from its capacious crop and beak to save them. (This is an interesting parallel to the Christian symbol of the pelican feeding its young in a spirit of self-sacrifice.) But birds, like humans, all had their faults and were destined to die, making it necessary to imagine an idealised, immortal bird to transcend them all. The simurgh was of Persian origin and like the phoenix was thought to plunge into the flames at the end of an era to renew itself. The simurgh also appeared as a redeemer, or at least a rescuer. In a seventeenth-century version of the *Fables of Pilpay*, known as *Anvar-i Suhayli*, the simurgh, with the glorious plumes of its tail fanned out across the sky, flies down surrounded by an army of other birds that have been summoned to rescue a nest of sandpipers washed down a river (see p. 30). The simurgh was also perfectly capable of carrying humans. The Persian *Shahnameh* or Book of Kings related how Prince Zal, who was abandoned on a mountain (as princes sometimes are), was reared by a simurgh, who endowed him with a magic feather when he was restored to the world of humans, and again came to the rescue when summoned. In Indian legends the simurgh also rescued humans from misfortune; and in various Mughal miniatures the wondrous bird appeared flying over lush landscapes and distant cities with a tiny hero dangling from its claws.

The crow deciding
whether the owl should
lead the assembly of birds
A miniature painting from
Anvar-i Suhayli, a version of
the *Kalila va Dimna* fables,
India, 1610–11.

But in the most haunting of the stories relating to the simurgh, composed in Khurasan in Persia around 1200 by the Sufi poet Farid al-Din Attar, the bird itself does not appear. Once again the birds had gathered to decide who would be their king, and from this beginning the poem gained its title 'The Conference of the Birds'. The hoopoe suggested they seek out the legendary simurgh, and the arduous journey, during which many birds perished, became an allegory of the quest for enlightenment and union with God.

It was in China late one moonless night
The simurgh first appeared to mortal sight
It let a feather float down through the air
And rumours of its fame spread everywhere.

All souls, explained the hoopoe, carry the impression of this feather and yearn to return whence it came. But many of the unfortunate birds had a fault, which doomed their quest to failure. The nightingale was too engrossed in its earthly love for the rose; the falcon was too jealous of its liberty; the parrot simply wanted to ensure its immortality; the pigeon, the dove and the francolin were too self-absorbed – 'the self that whirlpool where our lives are wrecked'; the partridge was too homesick for his own hillside, the heron for his marsh and the owl for his ruins; the finch was too afraid ever to set out. Only thirty birds finally reached the court of the simurgh, and they were turned away. All they found was a lake, and while gazing at their own reflections they achieved oneness. Indeed simurgh in Persian could be understood as a word-play on 'thirty birds'.

In the Arab world the simurgh became confused with other mythical birds, including the rukh that could carry an elephant and travelled into European myth as the roc, which looked more like a vast eagle. There was also the swan phoenix, or *qaqnus*, with a beak like a reed pipe with thirty holes, every stop a different note, through which it moaned its plaintive song which roused birds and men to ecstasy, or caused them to fall senseless. As a seabird with claws and a hooked beak it may have been linked with the siren

OPPOSITE: The sandpipers on their nest on the water while the simurgh leads the army of birds to their rescue. A miniature painting from *Anvar-i Suhayli*, a version of the *Kalila va Dimna* fables, India, 1610–11.

ABOVE: 'The Conference of the Birds', *Mantiq al-Tayr*, miniature painting by Habib Allah, c.1600. Metropolitan Museum of Art, New York.

Swan phoenix from *Kitab Na-t al-hayawan*, a treatise on animals and the medical properties of the various parts of their bodies, compiled from works of Aristotle and Ibn Bakhtishu, 13th century.

whose enchanting song lured Greek sailors on to rocks. As a bird that built its nest of kindling wood (making a great commotion in the process) and then immolated itself to give birth to a baby *qaqnus*, it was a kind of phoenix. As it died it sang through the stops in its beak with irresistible grief and beauty, hence the link with the dying swan. 'The silver swan who living had no note/When death approached unlocked her silent throat,' wrote English composer Orlando Gibbons in a famous madrigal. This idea can be traced back at least as far as Aristotle (the founding father of both European and Arabic science): 'Swans are musical and sing mostly as death approaches, when they fly out to sea. Men sailing past the coast of Libya have seen many singing in mournful strains and have even seen some dying.' The myth may have arisen through confusion between the mute swan, which only grunts and hisses, and the Bewick and whooper swans, whose calls and wing-beats sound deeply evocative when a flock flies overhead. Or the song may indeed be a rare phenomenon, as recorded by the American zoologist Daniel Giraud Elliot in 1898, after shooting a swan:

> On receiving his wound his wings became fixed and he began at once his song which continued until the water was reached nearly a mile away. I am perfectly familiar with every note a swan is accustomed to utter but never before or since have I heard anything like those sung by this stricken bird. Most plaintive in character and musical in tone, it sounded at times like the soft running of notes in an octave. And as the sound was borne to us, mellowed by the distance, we stood astonished and could only exclaim, 'we have heard the song of a dying swan'.

Meanwhile in China, and it was to China that Attar traced the simurgh that let fall the mystic feather, the phoenix or *fenghuang* was a bird that appeared only in times of peace and prosperity (an auspicious creature being generally more highly prized in China than a mystic one). Together with the Chinese dragon, which is also lucky, they represented the

Bird of paradise from
Chorui Hiako Shiu, an album
of coloured drawings, Japan, c.1860–70.

Golden pheasant from
Chorui Hiako Shiu, an album
of coloured drawings, Japan, c.1860–70.

four elements air and fire, earth and water; and also the male/female yin/yang principle of harmony. When illustrated by Chinese and Japanese artists the *fenghuang* was a composite bird of many colours, with long legs like a crane, a glorious trailing tail and the head of a pheasant – certainly its closest resemblance was to a green or golden pheasant, these being among the most emblematic and frequently illustrated of Oriental birds. However, the fascination with birds of paradise, which caused them to be traded across the China Sea long before Europeans heard tell of them, may have linked them too with the appearance of the *fenghuang*.

Albums and series of bird paintings and prints were precious possessions in China and Japan and nearly all artists turned their hands to them whatever their main speciality. So did the eighteenth-century artist Kitagawa Utamaro, the most sensual of the great Japanese printmakers. His most erotic series of prints was entitled 'Poems from the Pillow', and he was famed for his female beauties in intricately patterned kimonos, the geishas of the Floating World (or more specifically the brothels of the Yoshiwara district of Edo). In another series of prints entitled 'Twelve Hours in the Green Houses', Utamaro depicted himself painting a phoenix in one of the brothels, with the courtesans crowding to watch him (opposite). What would the Sufi poet have made of this manifestation of his mystic simurgh?

There is, however, a kind of mysticism in the very process of Chinese and Japanese painting. Capturing the spirit of a subject, for instance a bird on a branch (see p. 36), meant not merely depicting it accurately but becoming the bird and the branch, the wind in the leaves and the call of the bird. This involved endless practice, akin to meditation or martial arts, sometimes observing nature but more often copying the work of earlier artists. The albums of the Ten Bamboo Studio, from which this bird (overleaf) is taken, were manuals of painting and calligraphy produced and printed around 1630 by a group of artists in Nanjing, to be used in this way as copybooks. With assiduous technique an artist became so adept in the calligraphic style of handling brush, ink and paint that finally the bird was summoned into being

by meditating on the paper and moving the loaded brush deftly across it. This laughing thrush would be instantly recognisable by its white crest, the black band across its eyes, and the small fluffy way that it perches, tail down for balance; while the open beak would evoke the chuckling call for which it was named. There was a particularly allusive quality in monochrome ink and wash painting because of its link with calligraphy, where a skilled practitioner could form the characters in such a way that they hinted at extra meanings or deft visual puns. In the case of birds these might suggest flight, freedom or a specific symbolism such as the longevity associated with cranes, or married bliss represented (however misguidedly) by ducks and geese.

There may be a Buddhist allusion behind this dramatic Japanese album painting, which in the accompanying calligraphy is entitled *Eagle* (see p. 37). There are no black eagles in Japan, although the black cinereous vulture is familiar across Asia and is variously known as the monk vulture or holy eagle. If this represents a holy eagle, it is a reference to Mount Gridhrakuta, the Vulture Peak of Madhyar Pradesh in northern India, where, above miles of winding rock paths, Japanese Buddhist pilgrims have built a huge stupa. They were following in the footsteps of the great fifth-century Chinese Buddhist monk Fa-hsien (the model for Tripitaka in the popular story of Monkey) who travelled in search of authentic Buddhist texts, and described the night he spent meditating on Vulture Peak:

> There is a cavern in the rocks facing south in which Buddha himself sat in meditation. To the northwest there is another cave where Ananda was sitting when Mara the Lord of Misfortune assumed the form of a vulture and settled in front of the cave, frightening the disciple. Then Buddha made a cleft in the rock, put his hand through, and touched Ananda's shoulder so that his fear immediately left him. The footprints of the bird, and the cleft for Buddha's hand, are still there and hence comes the name of Vulture Peak.

Utamaro decorating the
interior of a 'Green House'
with a painting of a giant phoenix,
watched by admiring courtesans.
From *Seirō ehon nenjū gyōji*,
'Picture-book of Annals in the
Green Houses', by Jippensha Ikku,
illustrated by Utamaro, 1804.

Mount Gridhrakuta remains a habitat for thousands of vultures, which in India are regarded as purifiers. In Buddha's *Lotus Sutra* the mountain is referred to as the Pure Land: 'when the living have become faithful, honest and gentle, and want to see the Buddha even at the cost of their own lives, then together with the assembly of monks I will appear on Holy Eagle Peak'. At this point the inspiration of the vulture and the simurgh come curiously close.

The sumptuously illustrated albums (see p. 38) made for the Mughal emperors of India were mostly filled with intricate and brilliantly coloured illustrations of their own exploits, but they also contain pages that suggest their appreciation of pretty birds. Babur, the sixteenth-century founder of the dynasty, was characterised by his love of gardens almost as much as his conquests. In his memoirs, the *Baburnama*, compiled in the reign of his grandson Akbar around 1590, pages of battles alternate with studies of birds, flowers and trees, and their design evokes the Islamic gardens Babur created. Lines of decorative script divide the page, like rills of water running between the palms and fruit trees, as the rivers of Eden divided the original paradise garden. Bright flowers bloom in their shade, while birds peck and perch and sing among them – here magpies, redstarts and swifts, on other pages parrots, peacocks and partridges, mynah birds and ducks. Akbar's son Jahangir (r. 1605–27) became a fervent naturalist with a menagerie of exotic birds and animals in the grounds of his palace in Agra, and an agent stationed in Goa with instructions to examine every ship coming into port to search for more rarities. His main providers were the Dutch and Portuguese, but Jahangir also opened relations with the British East India Company. His court artist Ustad Mansur recorded his collections in the *Memoirs* of Jahangir, and they included a turkey brought all the way from America and a dodo from Mauritius.

The trade in birds also went the other way. George Edwards in his *Natural History of Uncommon Birds* (1743) recorded the birds arriving from the East as enthusiastically as those from across the Atlantic:

LEFT: Bird and bamboo.
Album leaf from the Ten Bamboo Studio collection of calligraphy and painting, c.1633. British Museum.

ABOVE: Vulture from *Chorui Hiako Shiu*, an album of coloured drawings, Japan, c.1860–70.

I have been collecting for more than twenty years and have been employed by many curious gentlemen in London to draw such rare foreign birds as they were possessed of, and took draughts for my own collection. I have not had the advantage of being in the countries where any of the birds I have described are found, but they are done from life with such facts as I had, and I have for variety's sake given them as many different turns and attitudes as I could devise.

Edwards painted Chinese pheasants from the collection of Hans Sloane, and mynah birds

brought to us by the India Company ships. For whistling, singing and talking they are accounted of the first rank, expressing words with an accent nearer human than parrots or any other birds taught to talk. The smaller bird I found at a dealer in curious birds in White-hart Yard in the Strand, the greater belonged to Dr George Wharton, treasurer of the College of Physicians.

From Bengal into the collection of Dr Mead, physician to the king, came a horned Indian pheasant 'most rare', a little black and orange hawk 'absolutely non-descript' (meaning never previously described), and a golden oriole (although Edwards knew they could be seen in southern Europe). The most spectacular of the live birds from Asia that Edwards painted was the cockatoo 'drawn from a bird shown at Bartholomew Fair'. Cockatoos were brought back by ships passing through the Indonesian Straits and Edwards heard that 'the Portuguese carry them to China and those people

LEFT: From top to bottom: Indian tree-pie (*Dendrocitta ruffa*), redstarts, Kirich (*Cypselus affinis*). Miniature painting from *Baburnama*, 'The Memoirs of Babur', c.1590–93.

OPPOSITE: Greater cockatoo from *A Natural History of Uncommon Birds*, by George Edwards, 1743.

J Edwards

160

Psittacus cristatus

give good rates for them'. Small wonder that 'at Makassar there are a great many of these sorts of birds they call cacatua, all white with a beak like a parrot and easily made tame and taught to talk. When they stand upon their guard they are very sightly for they spread a tuft of feathers that is on their heads and look most lovely'. But cockatoos occur naturally only in Australasia, to the east of the line that Alfred Wallace was to describe some hundred years later. Like the ill-fated birds of paradise (that George Edwards could depict only from stuffed and legless specimens in the cabinets of the rich) cockatoos were captured and widely dispersed on account of their exotic beauty.

James Forbes was born in the same decade that George Edwards published *Uncommon Birds* and, leaving home at sixteen, he spent most of his working life in India as a collector of revenues for the East India Company administration. There he observed oriental birds at first hand and recorded their natural lives. He watched tailor birds nesting in his garden in Bombay and later wrote in his *Oriental Memoirs* (published in 1813): 'it first selects a plant with large leaves and then gathers cotton from the cotton shrub, spins it to a thread by means of its long bill and slender feet, and then as with a needle sews the leaves neatly together to conceal its nest'. Still more intricate were the nests of the baya birds, or bottle-nested yellow sparrows; sometimes hundreds of their nests could be seen in one tree, made of long grasses woven together in the shape of a bottle gourd and suspended by threads from branches too slender for a snake or any other predator to reach. The nest had a little penthouse to deflect rain, and two compartments which the birds entered through holes at its wide base, one for the hen to incubate, another where the male could perch and entertain her 'with his chirping notes during her material

OPPOSITE: Spotted kingfisher from *Oriental Memoirs* by James Forbes, 1813.

duties'. The Indians, wrote Forbes, were very fond of these birds and taught them to fetch and carry: 'when the young women resort to the public fountains their lovers teach their baya birds to pluck the golden ornaments from the forehead of their favourite and bring it to their waiting master'. The most romantic of all birds was the nightingale. Forbes knew it was celebrated in oriental poetry 'for the plaintive sweetness of its song and its supposed passion for the rose'. Forbes mentioned the Persian poet Hafiz, who was most admired for combining love lyrics with intellectual hints at Sufi mysticism: 'Last night from the cypress branch the nightingale sang/In old Persian notes the lesson of spiritual journeys'. Forbes did not mention Omar Khayyam, Hafiz's more rumbustuous predecessor, who had not yet been popularised by Edward Fitzgerald: 'in divine/High piping Pehlevi with wine, wine, wine,/Red wine, the nightingale cries to the rose/that sallow cheek of hers t'incarnadine'.

As he was waiting on the Malabar coast for his vessel to finish loading pepper, before he finally left India, Forbes saw the candidate for his last and loveliest bird plate – the spotted kingfisher – which he caught in action as it dived downwards from a rush. The halcyon was normally a good omen but, wrote Forbes, 'every rural excursion and social pleasure was tinged with gloom for our unfortunate countrymen in the dominions of Tipu Sultan'. Forbes described the Black Hole of Calcutta, forced marches of roped prisoners, and Tipu's mechanical tiger tearing and growling at the throat of an English officer. It is a reminder that the delights of birdwatching were sometimes snatched from the jaws of danger.

It was probably another officer of the East India Company, returning home and selling off specimens of Indian birds, who first inspired John Gould to create the *Gould Folios* – large ornithologies with beautiful hand-coloured lithographs (the first was *Birds of the Himalayas* in 1832) that eventually encompassed whole continents as well as individual bird families such as toucans and hummingbirds. In 1827, aged twenty-three, Gould had gained a post at the newly founded London Zoo as taxidermist and curator

ABOVE: Red-eared finches from
The Birds of Australia by John Gould,
1848–69.

OPPOSITE: Yellow-legged spoonbill
from *The Birds of Australia* by John Gould,
1848–69.

of birds and, most importantly, had married his loyal wife Elizabeth, a better artist than he and the lithographer of all his plates (until she died after giving birth to their eighth child in 1841). Gould was blessed with the prodigious energy that characterised successful Victorians, otherwise he could never have become such a global ornithologist, let alone a profitable publisher. His greatest work was *Birds of Australia*, a subject which at that time was virtually undocumented. Gould first started the project after receiving some bird skins from his wife's brothers, who had emigrated to Australia, but he soon realised he would lack authority unless he travelled to Australia himself (with wife, family and an assistant who was later killed by Aborigines). Funded by the profits from previous works they intrepidly set sail in 1838, returning two years later with the first live budgerigars (the 'little warbling grass parakeets' which 'differ from all others in having the most animated and pleasing song'). Back in London Gould immediately started to publish *Birds of Australia*.

Gould had also been inspired by Charles Darwin, who had returned from the *Beagle* voyage in 1836, and turned to Gould with the puzzle of his finches and other matters ornithological, including the birds he had seen in Australia. Indeed there were finches there too, including the Gouldian finch which was first collected by Benjamin Bynoe the surgeon on HMS *Beagle*, although Gould named it in honour of his wife after she died ('while cheerfully engaged in illustrating the present work'). Gould remarked, in Darwinian mode, that the red-eared finch with a blunt bill must be able to feed differently from the painted finch with a pointed beak. Later, in the introduction to the supplement which was published in 1869, Gould marvelled not only over the birds which were there – cockatoos, honeyeaters, emus, cassowaries (and he paid due tribute to Wallace's discovery of distinct Australasian species), but he also discussed those birds that were not in Australia. No hornbills 'because there are none of the large fruit-bearing trees which occur in India and Africa, and which are so essential to the existence of these birds'. No woodpeckers

'because the bark of the trees is not adapted for the shelter of insects on which they feed'. No vultures 'probably because there were no horses, cows or antelope' in Australia.

There were intermediate species of birds that faced Gould with evolutionary queries, such as the yellow-legged spoonbill (see p. 43), which was illustrated in a most atmospheric setting of river and jungle (surely an inspiration for Henri Rousseau's 1907 painting *The Snake Charmer*). This spoonbill has a narrower bill than others and seems closer to an ibis, especially the Australian straw-necked ibis, which has similar plumes gracing its neck. Probably this is an early offshoot from the ancestry of other spoonbills, but close enough to belong to the same genus. Around the edge of that specialised bill are lines of sensors. With these a spoonbill moves slowly through the shallows, stirring up the mud and sweeping its bill from side to side, feeling for signs of life to eat.

Also distinct to Australasia are the honeyeaters and wattlebirds, a large and diverse group, but all characterised by their brush-tipped tongues which are frayed and fringed with bristles to suck up nectar as they flip them rapidly and frequently into flowers. A great many Australasian plants are fertilised by honeyeaters, including protea, myrtle, eucalyptus and banksia, all of which complement the birds with extraordinary brush-like flower-parts. Many honeyeaters follow the flowering of their favourite food plants, arriving in flocks when the moment is right. They are not solely reliant on nectar because they supplement their diet with sugary resins as well as berries and insects. Honeyeaters do not hover as they feed, and although in other ways they look and behave much like sunbirds and hummingbirds (the nectar feeders of Africa and America) they are not related, being an example of convergent evolution in quite separate places.

Much as Gould relished and recorded all that was amazingly different in Australia, it was heart-warming for him, as for many a settler, to see that here too robins and wrens inhabited the gardens. The blue wren is really a bright little warbler, but it behaves like a wren and the female at least is the familiar brown. As Gould wrote, 'their mode of progression can scarcely be called running, it is rather a succession of bounding hops performed with great rapidity ... while thus employed its tail is carried perpendicularly or thrown forward over the back ... their song is a hurried strain somewhat like the wren of Europe'. In winter blue wrens are tame and familiar but in the breeding season they grow shy, although Gould noted that they built their nests in populous places such as the Botanic Gardens in Sydney and the Colonial Secretary's Office. The Australian robin seemed another link with home (apart from its yellow breast) as it landed on stumps 'raising its tail at the moment of perching' and 'looked with a sprightly air'.

OPPOSITE: Helmeted honeyeaters on banksia from the supplement to *The Birds of Australia* by John Gould, 1848–69.

CHAPTER THREE

Freedom, Hunting and Captivity

Nothing can express freedom like a bird wheeling against the sky – or flitting, hovering, mounting, flapping – in a flight pattern peculiarly and touchingly its own. Although we cannot fly, our thoughts can; so it is small wonder that poets and artists find bird allusions irresistible. If a bird also sings, another of our senses is enchanted and, being the only other creatures that can make melodies, we identify birdsong as another sign of joyous freedom (although to the bird it may be anything but). Our responses come from knowing that freedom owes its intensity to the existence of its opposite, and birds embody this too and react to it with every instinct. Consider the opening to Siegfried Sassoon's poem 'Everyone Sang', which is far more poignant than joyous since it described the trenches in the First World War: an experience that Sassoon (despite his bravery) normally wrote of with bitterness and loathing. It is uncertain whether the poem was about the soldiers of his regiment, spontaneously raising their spirits before an engagement, or the combined armies hearing of armistice:

Everyone suddenly burst out singing
And I was filled with such delight
As prisoned birds must find in freedom
Winging wildly across the white
Orchards and dark green fields; on; on; and out of sight.

It might even describe the souls of the dead:

… Everyone
Was a bird; and the song was wordless; the singing will never be done.

The story of Noah's Ark is very similar, telling of lone survivors in a world of death, and the image of the birds and animals being released as the floods receded was a major symbol of deliverance. To express this, here a duck is held out tenderly, preparing to take flight from the hands of Noah's wife. The dove with its olive branch and several other birds are lifting their wings on the free air, while the peacock, stork, cockerel and green goshawk strut away. The curiosity of the story has made it a great favourite, and in the fifteenth-century devotional book known as the *Bedford Hours* it opens the whole sequence of prayers, which is unusual, and suggests (because there are two miniatures, the other of building the Ark) that the flood story held some special importance for the Duke of Bedford when he commissioned the book. In 1422, the year before the book was made, he had become Regent of France when his brother Henry V died, and he had claimed the French throne on behalf of his baby nephew Henry VI. The Duke held Paris (where this manuscript was made for him by the finest illuminators) and his armies controlled large tracts of France (Joan of Arc did not appear to rally the French until 1429). At this auspicious moment, did the Duke fancy himself redeemed as Noah was; and did he hope the dove with the olive branch represented the final outcome of his own efforts?

Many centuries of human imaginative identification with birds, freedom and flight never prevented birds being the victims of captivity and slaughter. Before anything else men were hunters, succeeding through their speed, stamina and cunning, and from ancient times people hunted not only for subsistence, but also for recreation. So the joy that birds inspire can also be seen through this spectrum, in artistic depictions of hunting scenes. Nebamun hunting in the marshes, an ancient Egyptian tomb painting from around 1350 BC, shows the deceased among the teeming bird life on the banks of the Nile, as if he is forever enjoying the sports of his prime. In one hand he holds a decoy in the form of pintail ducks and, as he raises his throwing stick to catapult them, the startled birds – geese, ducks and wagtails – rise up among the papyrus reeds, beating their wings to escape. The

OPPOSITE: Noah's Ark from the *Bedford Hours*, c.1423.

48

ABOVE: Nebamun fowling and fishing
in the marshes. Wall painting from the
tomb of Nebamun, Thebes, Egypt,
c.1350 BC. British Museum.

BELOW: Flying crane in
moonlight from *Kyomjae hwachop*,
'Album of paintings by Kyomjae',
Korea, c.1900.

tawny hunting cat has leapt up to catch no fewer than three
birds. But one egret faces Nebamun with surprising calm,
and a red Egyptian goose on the prow of his ship remains
perfectly still (possibly it was a tame bird used as a decoy).
Beneath them the water is full of fish and lotus flowers
(and a spear from the missing fishing scene originally
depicted below is just visible). The wildlife may be realistic
but Nebamun is not – Egyptian men did not go hunting
with their decorative womenfolk clutching flowers. This is
an idyll of the afterlife. On its way between this world and
the next the Egyptian soul passed through the reed beds and,
having survived testing ordeals, hoped sometimes to revisit
the haunts of its earthly existence in the form of a bird.
The whole scene, with the cat and the poisonous puffer
fish beneath it, may also contain a warning to the
bird/soul to be wary.

A love of hunting pervaded most cultures. In
thirteenth-century China, Marco Polo described Kublai
Khan (the Mongol Emperor of China) setting forth to
hunt in

a wooden pavilion mounted on the backs of four
elephants. On the outside, the pavilion was handsomely
carved and hung with lion skins, inside it was lined
with cloth of gold. With him in the pavilion the Great
Khan carried twelve of his best gerfalcons and twelve
officers. Those riding on horseback beside the pavilion
told him of the approach of cranes and other birds,
upon which he raised a curtain and gave directions to
the officers to let fly the gerfalcons. They seized the
cranes and overpowered them after a long struggle. The
Great Khan viewed this sport as he lay upon his couch
and it afforded extreme satisfaction to his Majesty.

OPPOSITE: Timur hunting near
Multan from *Zafarnama of Sharaf
al-Din*, Shiraz, 1533.

OPPOSITE: Babur and the bird-catchers of Kabul from *Baburnama*, 'The Memoirs of Babur', Mughal, 1590–93.

A century later his barbaric kinsman Timur (or Tamerlane) tried but failed to reconquer China; nor could he emulate Kublai's hunting pavilion mounted on elephants, his skill being the more ancient Mongol tradition of horseback fighting and massacre. Yet Timur remained a hero in the Islamic world of Central Asia, as this sixteenth-century Persian manuscript testifies. His hunting scene encompasses several kinds of deer, a buffalo and a leopard being intrepidly speared from horseback (see p. 51); but against the golden sky Timur is hawking, and beautiful peacocks fly up in alarm.

Another century had passed when Timur's descendant Babur, whose restless Mongol heritage caused him to advance south from Kabul with conquering armies, founded the Mughal dynasty of India. He too was celebrated in hunting and battle scenes, but among the luxuriant images in the memoirs of Babur (*Baburnama*) there is one enchantingly different miniature with many birds. Babur is accompanied by the bird-catchers of Kabul, who are trapping pretty birds for the aviaries of the gardens that he loved. (Later Babur's great-grandson Jahangir was to be the most avid bird collector of the dynasty.) The emperor's favourite hawk is being held ready by a retainer; perhaps it will be let loose to sport among the ducks a little later, but the present image shows the decoys at work behind their hides and trees, with food and bird sounds and traps at the ready.

Only one European hunting scene from a medieval Italian manuscript shows a comparable profusion of birds. The Cocharelli *Treatise on the Seven Vices* was produced in Genoa late in the fourteenth century as a moral instruction book for the younger members of the Cocharelli family. Among the predictable warnings against drinking, gambling and money-lending there are evocative illustrations of wholesome occupations, including the men of the family riding out to hunt, falcons on wrists, hounds panting, and flocks of birds overhead. White storks with black-tipped wings get noisily airborne, busy little partridges take flight – and, in the opposite direction, even plumper red-legged partridges. Still resting in the trees are a blue tit, a jay and two hoopoes. Down the left-hand margin ducks tumble

and quack as a hawk attacks their leader; in the central margin magpies fly off and goldfinches flutter. On the right, two hawks attack a crane and a pheasant, while on the rocks beneath an eagle has a nest with young. At the top of the page is a scene of carnage, in which carrion crows feast on a dead fox, a vulture swallows the entrails of a deer and two kites fly in for the feast.

The definitive treatise on falconry, which was referred to by Cocharelli and many others, was produced in Italy. It was written by Frederick II (d. 1250), Stupor Mundi, Holy Roman Emperor, King of Sicily and Jerusalem and scourge of the Pope, who had a passion for all aspects of the sport. The heart of his empire was Sicily, where Arabic influence was strong and included Oriental techniques in falconry. Frederick maintained up to fifty falcons, rearing his own and collecting new breeds – his letters survive requesting arctic gerfalcons from Greenland – besides which he also had a menagerie of exotic birds. Frederick's treatise *De arte venandi cum avibus* defined the standards of this unique way of hunting with trained birds, and was widely read and translated. Frederick dealt scientifically with all aspects of their care and training, based on his own long experience and observation (including how to take young birds from the nest). There were also translated excerpts from Arabic works on falconry and Aristotle's ornithological observations.

Against the background of this sport of kings, the English author Geoffrey Chaucer, who was not only a court poet but had travelled to Italy on diplomatic missions (acquainting himself with the works of Dante, Boccaccio and very possibly *De art venandi* and some oriental lore), produced his poem 'The Parliament of Fowls'. It was written around 1380 and possibly linked to the wedding of Richard II and Anne of Bohemia. Very different from Farid al-Din Attar's 'Conference of the Birds', which initiated the quest for the simurgh, it nevertheless began as a yearning for love and spiritual wisdom and led to 'a garden full of blossomy boughs'. Here all the birds were assembled on St Valentine's Day to choose a mate. Chaucer set the birds of prey highest in rank: 'the royal eagle that pierces the sun with his sharp

glance; the goshawk that harasses other birds with his fierce
ravening; the noble falcon that with his feet grasps the king's
hand; the bold sparrow hawk foe of quails; the merlin that
often greedily pursues the lark'. These were the Lords. The
Commons were the little birds that eat worms, together with
the waterfowl and birds that live on seed, 'so many that it was
a marvel to see'. The purpose of the assembly was to witness
a beautiful formel (young female) eagle choose a mate, and
three noble tercel (male) eagles stake their claims. There
followed a fine parliamentary skit on the behaviour and
opinion of various birds when faced with love's dilemmas,
until the formel eagle declared herself unable to choose
and was granted a year's grace. Chaucer's marvellous gift
of blending the serious and the absurd was mirrored in the
images known as drolleries which decorated the margins of
illuminated manuscripts. Surrounding prayers and religious
readings with rudery and humour, sometimes they made
punning reference to the text, or reflected a contemporary
grievance or innuendo. The *Luttrell Psalter* (a book of psalms),
from which this falconer is taken, is typically alive with
scenes of farming, feasting and pastimes. It was made for
Sir Geoffrey Luttrell, a Lincolnshire aristocrat, in the 1330s
(the age into which Chaucer was born). A rider hunting
with a hawk was recognised as an allegory of sexual pursuit
(as readers of 'The Parliament of Fowls' would have
appreciated) but here it could be a more complicated
reference to the parish priest of the church where the
Luttrell family worshipped. He owed a rent of a sparrowhawk
to his lord in return for the right to common pasture on the
estate, although not in the Luttrell parkland which had been
enclosed for hunting.

Such drolleries reflected a topsy-turvy world.
Sometimes birds hunted people, or shot one another with
arrows, and fun was poked at ordinary folk seen using
catapults, chasing crows from the fields or trapping birds.
The *Psalter* of Robert de Lisle (created in East Anglia around
1310) features a bird-catcher dressed in pink, hiding in a bush
and using an owl as a decoy. Other birds so detest owls that
they are liable, given half a chance, to mob them, and here the

OPPOSITE: Goshawk and sparrowhawk
from *The Birds of America* by
John James Audubon, 1827–38.

ABOVE: A hunter on horseback
from the *Luttrell Psalter*, c.1320–40.

te sanctus pro lege dei siu
tertauit uscp ad mortem et
a uerbis impior non timuit.
tundatus enim erat supra tir
mam petram. V. Corona au
rea super caput aus. expressa
signo sanditatis glorie horis.
Oremus: Corneli Alia an.

owl itself is both trapped and trapping. Among the mob the magpie is prominent (as the crow was the ringleader in the *Fables of Pilpay*). There are also jays, goldfinches, bullfinches and a blue tit. The bird-catcher's pole is either a part of his net or it may be covered in bird lime. Many little birds were caged either as songbirds, such as linnets and nightingales, or as pets, such as sparrows and finches, or parrots for the rich. In some manuscripts caged birds allude to the soul trapped in the body, or Jesus born as a human child. The *Hours* of Catherine of Cleves, a richly decorated manuscript made in the Netherlands in the mid-fifteenth century, has two borders with bird cages. In one a bird-trapper stretches out strings to catch tits, while the accompanying miniature shows an angel releasing souls from the jaws of hell. The other border is bizarrely beautiful, typical of this Renaissance period of

OPPOSITE: Saints Cornelius and Cyprian within a border of bird cages from the *Hours* of Catherine of Cleves, Utrecht, c.1440. The Pierpont Morgan Library, New York.

ABOVE: Hunter using an owl as a decoy, from the Psalter of Robert de Lisle, c.1310.

artistic experiment with realism, but unique in surrounding the page with gilded cages: there are no fewer than eight and all are different. One is a training device with perches and tiny buckets on chains, where the bird learned to tip the bucket and drink the water inside – perhaps here a symbol of spiritual purification. Two others, a long spiralling cage and a revolving drum, were presumably designed to discourage flight. Were these cages allegories of the trials of the soul in this earthly life? Or did Catherine Duchess of Cleves (whose initials appear on one of the cage covers) simply collect caged birds? Two centuries later, when caged or escaping birds frequently appeared alongside pretty girls in paintings of Dutch interiors, they had become symbols of seduction and lost virginity.

In the mid-twentieth century the French poet Jacques Prévert wrote a surreal poem, 'To paint the portrait of a bird', which echoes the conflicting fascination and cruelty of human attempts to relate to birds (and each other):

'First paint a cage with an open door. Then place the canvas against a tree and wait. It may be many years before the bird arrives. When it does, keep a profound silence while the bird enters the cage, then gently close the door with a brush and paint out the bars, without touching any of the feathers of the bird. Then the artist must paint green foliage and the wind's freshness and the noise of insects in the summer heat. If the bird sings it is a good sign, a sign the painting is good. Then the artist may gently pull out one of the bird's feathers and sign the picture.'

Most birds were fair game when it came to caging or killing, and in some cases those with the sweetest song or the most succulent flesh were provided with excellent camouflage: the insignificant linnet; the gently striped woodcock who searches for food among the damp woodland leaves; the mottled quail lurking in the tawny grass; and the snipe among the reeds of marshland; the dappled browns of their feathers and their plump vulnerability are all perfectly captured in the *Sherborne Missal*. The snipe has an added advantage if its cover is sprung because its erratic flight pattern makes it very hard to aim at (hence the term 'sniper' for a skilled marksman). During the seventeenth century, shooting with guns gradually superseded hawking and birds were more rapidly destroyed. In contemporary still-life paintings with game, the feathered carnage bore testimony to the relish engendered by this sport. New game laws sought to control the numbers slain by restricting hunting rights to the wealthy landed classes, while outlawing the rural classes who might actually need the food. What was Rembrandt van Rijn saying when he painted a self-portrait in 1639, holding up a dead bittern, a bird already threatened by over-hunting and the draining of the marshes? His own face is in deep shadow while the light shines on the dappled plumage of the bird, an exquisite example of Rembrandt's method of highlighting a mystery. Perhaps it was an allegory of life and death; or Rembrandt's attempt to reach the aristocratic heights of those licensed to hunt bittern; or alternatively, a protest at injustice.

As Europeans explored and colonised new continents, their hunting instincts found fresh outlets. In India in 1779, the artist James Forbes joined an excursion of the Nerbudda

ABOVE: Snipe from the *Sherborne Missal*, c.1399–1407.

OPPOSITE: Florican from *Oriental Memoirs* by James Forbes, 1813.

The CURMOOR or FLORICAN,
one of the highest flavoured Birds in India.

of Guzerat into the wilds; he did not much relish hunting but there was no way he could go alone. He was thus able to watch 'fourteen kinds of duck some very lovely, pelicans, spoonbills, white and rose flamingos, storks, cranes and many aquatic birds in lakes and marshes, woodcocks, snipe and partridge'. But above these, 'the florican exceeds all Indian wildfowl in delicacy of flavour; its varied plumage, lofty carriage and tuft of black feathers falling gracefully from its head make him one of the most elegant birds in India'. Hawking had originated in the East and remained a sport there after guns had made it obsolete in the West. But images of the magnificent birds of prey owned by the Indian rajahs or Japanese samurai emphasised the supreme irony of their situation: these monarchs of the sky who had been made captive, their cruelty curbed for man's sport and their freedom utterly compromised.

According to Pliny the Elder, the first person to devise a cage for wild fowl was M. Laevius Strabo, a Roman with a villa in Brindisi who maintained an aviary 'to keep fowls within narrow coops and cages as prisoners, to which creatures nature had allowed the wide air for their scope and habitation'. But the most wondrous and ill-fated were the aviaries of Tenochtitlan belonging to Moctezuma, the Aztec ruler of Mexico at the moment when the Spaniards arrived in 1519. There were of course intimations of what awaited Hernán Cortés and his rugged entourage as they came up from the coast and saw the wild birds around them: first, graceful white egrets, then small flashes of brilliant colour from hummingbirds and flycatchers, or extraordinary perched forms of toucans and macaws, while overhead hovered birds of prey and brooding condors. Moctezuma was disturbed by the news of Cortés' approach but he sent a welcoming party, led by the princely Cacama, who greeted them from a litter decorated with gold, gems and the green plumes of the quetzal bird. When the Spaniards first saw Moctezuma himself he was shaded by a canopy of intricate feather-work (made by the women of the court, who also created fairy-like cloaks and headdresses by embroidering feathers on to thin cotton webbing). The sacred crown of

ABOVE: Captive hawk from *Nigri kobushi*, 'The Clenched Fist', a manual of falconry, Japan, c.1750.

OPPOSITE: Hawk flying free from *Nigri kobushi*, 'The Clenched Fist', a manual of falconry, Japan, c.1750.

Moctezuma was made from 400 feathers of the quetzal bird. The number represented eternity and the bird represented wisdom, fertility, freedom and peace. Its green feathers also adorned the images of the snake god of the Mayans and Aztecs, Quetzalcoatl, a monstrous deity of the air who wore the quetzal bird with its head behind his own, its wings across his shoulders and the green plumes of its tail hanging to the ground.

Bernal Diaz, who accompanied Cortés, wrote in his account:

> When we saw those cities and villages built on the water, and that straight and level causeway leading to Mexico [Tenochtitlan – now Mexico City] we were astounded, it seemed like an enchanted vision, this first glimpse of things never heard of, seen or dreamed of before ... the palaces in which they lodged us, the

orchard and the garden, the diversity of trees, the paths choked with flowers and the pond of fresh water where birds of many varieties come.

Moctezuma's own palace had hundreds of rooms, courtyards with fountains, botanic gardens and latticed aviaries in ten sections with 300 servants to care for the hundreds of birds they contained. Even Cortés, who was intensely occupied with the politics of conquest, noticed the birds and wrote to Charles V describing them, saying that there was nothing like this in Europe: 'everything from the royal eagle and other birds of great size down to tiny birds of many-coloured plumage'. Bernal Diaz elaborated: 'Parrots of many colours, beautifully marked ducks, and birds with long stilted legs with body, wings and tail all red.' There were also blue-throated hummingbirds, vermilion flycatchers, copper-tailed trogons, green jays and summer tanagers, wrens and thrushes.

Aztec warriors with feathered
headdresses and shields from
a copy of the *Lienzo de Tlaxcalla*
by Diego Muñoz Camargo, c.1585.

Short-billed toucan from
A Monograph on the Ramphastidæ
by John Gould, 1834.

But by 1520 Moctezuma had the measure of the grasping Spaniards and he banished them from the city. Within a year they were back, relentless and vengeful, to destroy what Cortés himself had described as the most beautiful city in the world. Diaz concluded his lyrical descriptions 'today all that I saw is overthrown and destroyed, nothing is left standing'. In his 1843 book *History of the Conquest of Mexico*, William Prescott gave the tragic details of the burning of the aviaries:

> On the other side of the square adjoining Montezuma's residence was the House of Birds filled with specimens of all the painted varieties which swarmed over the wide forests of Mexico. It was an airy and elegant building of wood and bamboo. The torches were applied and the fanciful structure was soon wrapped in flames that sent their baleful splendours far and wide over city and lake. Its feathered inhabitants either perished in the fire, or those of strong wing, bursting the burning lattice work of the aviary, soared high into the air and fluttering for a while over the city fled with loud screams to their native forests beyond the mountains.

('Montezuma' is a common European misspelling.) As if in epitaph one fascinating chestnut-coloured bird was named *Montezuma oropendola* (Montezuma's golden pendulum). The courtship display of the male starts with bowing. Then he swings by his feet with a song that bubbles and gurgles, while spreading out the shining yellow feathers of his tail, like a golden pendulum. The high-security nests that he builds are intricately woven sacks which hang 3 feet (1 metre) or more from the branches to which they are fixed. Often they are built near large wasps' nests so that the insects' stinging will deter predators. Small wonder that birds have been regarded as allegorical beings.

Quetzal from *A Monograph on the Trogonidæ* by John Gould, 1838.

63

CHAPTER FOUR

Winged Spirits and Messengers

Angels and birds have an obvious winged affinity – nowhere better expressed than in this biblical image of the Apocalypse. It depicts the moment when seven angels had finished pouring out the vials of God's wrath upon the wicked, who had oppressed and seduced his people. Next came the final war of destruction which made way for a new heaven and a new earth. As a prelude there appeared 'an angel standing in the sun, and he cried with a loud voice calling all the fowls that fly in mid-heaven "come and gather yourselves together unto the supper of the great God"' (Revelation 19.17). Their vengeful meal was to consist of the flesh of the defeated, but here the artist preferred to convey a glorious vision of the angel's summons to the birds; nor, apart from the magpie, are there any carrion birds. The dramatic red circles behind the angel represent the rays of the sun from which this dazzling vision emanated, and the stylised palm tree suggests the Middle Eastern land of Armageddon where God vented his wrath. But the birds, except for the parrot, were those familiar to the East Anglian artist illuminating this fourteenth-century manuscript: bullfinches and a goldfinch, a jay, a blue and green kingfisher, a finely marked woodcock, a black and white wading bird and a red-headed crane. Above them all on the top of the tree sits a tiny wren.

Wrens had form as the king of the birds:

The wren, the wren, the king of all birds
St Stephen's day he was caught in the furze
Although he is little his honour is great
Rise up kind sir and give us a treat …
Up with the kettle and down with the pan
Give us some money to bury the wren.

One story that attempted to explain how something so small became king of the birds claimed that, during the flying competition that decided the matter, the wren hid on the back of the eagle and when at last the eagle grew tired of soaring higher than all other birds, the wren popped out from the feathers on the eagle's back and flew a little higher.

Perhaps this proved the wren was the cleverest of birds, or perhaps it was once considered sacred. Wrens certainly inspired an impressive body of superstition, at the centre of which lay the wren-hunt, a midwinter ceremony from which the above verse derives. It is still surprisingly widespread in Europe and is now fixed either on Boxing Day, New Year's Day or Twelfth Night. First it involved the capture of the wren (nowadays an effigy), then the decoration of its cage or perch with evergreen leaves or ribbons. Sometimes the wren was treated as enormously heavy and placed on a float.

OPPOSITE: Wren from
the *Sherborne Missal*,
c. 1399–1407.

ABOVE: Angel with birds and
a rabbit from the Queen Mary
Apocalypse, c.1310–25.

Its parade was joined by disguised participants in straw suits, or men dressed as women, or mummers. Their performances might include mock battles, resurrections, hobby horses or fools with bladders on sticks, all typical of the medieval Feast of Fools (derived from the Roman festival of Saturnalia) when in midwinter the forces of darkness and infertility had to be overcome by inverting the normal order of things. In this context the diminutive size of the bird king was presumably the key to its choice. Another part of the spell was revelry, hence the plea from the agricultural workers who maintained these traditions: 'Give us some money to bury the wren.'

If such survivals suggest the wren was once an otherworldly bird linked with ancient cults, there was also a tradition that it haunted graveyards or, in the words of the Jacobean dramatist John Webster, 'o'er shady groves they

ABOVE: Sirens from *Li Livres dou Trésor* by Brunetto Latini, France, c.1315–25.

OPPOSITE: 'Queen of the Night', Babylonian, c.19th–18th century BC. British Museum, London.

hover, and with leaves and flowers do cover, the friendless bodies of unburied men' (*The White Devil*, 5.iv). Indeed wrens do shuffle and disappear among dead leaves and tiny crevices, and their capacity for loud scolding also earned them a reputation for betrayal – of Christ in the Garden of Gethsemane, or of St Stephen as he tried to escape martyrdom, or of Irish troops ambushing Cromwell. Not to be outdone, the Isle of Man cast the wren as a siren, once a beautiful enchantress with a sweet voice who lured men to perish at sea. She was transformed at last (by a knight errant of impeccable purity) into a wren, but every New Year's Day she returns as a fairy and is hunted. The earlier Sirens of Greek legend, who tried to lure Odysseus on to their rocks, generally had wings, but otherwise (like harpies) they were the antithesis of angels. They came to embody lustful temptation and continued to exercise a powerful fascination over the medieval mind. Were they beautiful or hideous, bird, fish or female? In a fourteenth-century version of Brunetto Latini's *Li Livres dou Trésor* (an early encyclopedia) the musical sirens were displayed at various stages of transformation, more intriguing than alluring. Their ancestry may be traceable via Greece to ancient Mesopotamia, where it was feared that the souls of the dead were like sad birds with flightless wings trapped in a dim and dusty underworld. The Mesopotamian goddess Ereshkigal was intent on luring victims to her realm, and in a glorious epic lament her sister goddess or alter ego Inanna (later called Ishtar) followed the lure, abandoning her veils and jewels seven times as she went through the seven gates of the Underworld and lay as one dead, awaiting her inevitable springtime rescue. It is uncertain whether the ancient Babylonian carving, now popularly known as the 'Queen of the Night', represents Ereshkigal (the owls suggest it), or Inanna/Ishtar (lions were her attribute) or the dual nature of one goddess. She is certainly an ancient manifestation of a powerful winged spirit, complete with the talons of a bird of prey and probably able to descend into hell or soar into heaven – which angels were also believed to do.

Such a heritage proves how fierce angels might be. After all, the fallen angel Lucifer ruled hell as the Devil

and the Archangel Michael and all good angels had to be strong enough to overcome him. But the favourite angels of imagination and of artistic tradition were the messenger angels, endowed with wings more magnificent than any bird, bringing glad tidings of great joy. They appear in countless paintings and miniatures announcing the birth of Christ, accompanied by the white dove of the Holy Spirit, which is either flying down the ray of light shining from God towards the Virgin Mary, or in the halo of light above her head. This scenario was established by long tradition, although the actual biblical references to the Holy Spirit descending in the form of a dove came not with the Annunciation but during the Baptism of Christ.

A white dove is more numinous, but it belongs to the same species as the rock dove, feral pigeon and domesticated carrier pigeon, *Columba livia*, and as messengers they have a long and distinguished history. The legendary ancestor figures Noah and Utnapishtim (the survivor of the original Mesopotamian flood epic) both used a dove and a raven to ascertain whether dry land had returned. On a more historical level carrier pigeons were used in the sixth century BC in the reign of King Cyrus of Persia, and by the ancient Greeks to spread news of the winners of the Olympic Games. Pigeons carried messages of conquest for Julius Caesar and Genghis Khan. Marco Polo mentioned their extensive use in the East; the Mughal emperors introduced pigeon breeding to India; and the Genoese used them in their medieval watchtowers around the Mediterranean. Whether news of the battle of Waterloo in 1815 was first brought to England by Rothschild's pigeon rather than Wellington's dispatch is disputed, but pigeons were certainly used by Paul Reuter, the nineteenth-century founder of Reuters press agency, and the first airmail stamp was created for pigeon post in New Zealand in 1899, to fly between Auckland and Great Barrier Island. During the First and Second World Wars pigeons were trained to carry messages back to their home coop behind the lines, which they did heroically even as enemy soldiers shot at them. One, called Mocker, flew fifty-two missions before being wounded, and Cher Ami, who was

ABOVE: The Annunciation, illumination by Gerard Horenbout from the *Sforza Hours*, c.1517–20.

OPPOSITE: Pigeons in Mughal India, miniature painting from *Kabutar-nama*, India, 1788.

posthumously decorated, survived to the last week of the war in 1918 when he lost a foot and an eye but still delivered his message, saving a large group of American soldiers trapped behind enemy lines. In the Second World War pigeons were used both during the Normandy invasion and the Arnhem landings. How did they do it? Their skill is due to a kind of homing device, although if their home and their food are based in two different places they can be trained to accomplish round trips of up to 100 miles (160 km). Modern science is still a little puzzled by how this is achieved. Pigeons can detect the earth's magnetic field because on top of their beak is a concentration of iron particles which remain aligned to the north and act as a compass for them. As they come nearer home their senses of sight and smell help them to navigate, but different colonies respond differently when these reactions are tested. It is this wide capacity for variation which has fascinated those who breed pigeons, whether for fancy appearance or for competitive racing. It also brought pigeons to Darwin's attention in the 1850s. Although his West Indian finches and mockingbirds had first set his

ABOVE: Great Barrier Island one-shilling pigeongram, 1899.

OPPOSITE: The ascent to heaven of the Prophet Muhammad, guided by the Archangel Gabriel, with an escort of angels, from Nizami's *Khamsa* (Five Poems), Iran, 1539–43.

theorising in motion, Darwin realised that homely pigeons were excellent candidates for experimental breeding, enabling him to test scientifically for evolutionary variation. He therefore set up his own pigeon loft and joined the historic legions of pigeon fanciers.

The other characteristics of doves and pigeons that have enchanted generations are their fluttering, cooing gentleness and amorous antics; they even touch beaks in a kiss. They have been regarded as love birds at least since the Old Testament Song of Songs – 'Behold thou art fair my beloved, behold thou art fair, thou hast dove's eyes' – and behind that refrain lurk the love and fertility goddesses of the ancient Near East and Mediterranean. Inanna, Ishtar, Astarte, Aphrodite, right through to Venus – all had doves as their emblem. Islam inherited the symbolic link between doves and divine love, and flocks are encouraged to flutter around some of the holiest mosques. Islam also has angels. The angel Gabriel appeared before Muhammad as he did before the Virgin Mary, although with a different summons. This led the Prophet to undertake the Night Journey, mounted on a white mule called Buraq – who sometimes has wings and sometimes a peacock's tail – and with a wondrous escort of angels. Muhammad ascended above the clouds enclosed in holy fire. Some images of the Night Journey show the constellations and the seven circles of heaven where, at each of the seven gates, the Prophet's identity was challenged and Gabriel guided him through. Finally Muhammad met with Allah and was given prayers to be said fifty times a day. But as he came away Moses warned him that his followers would never achieve such a feat, so Muhammad returned to Allah and bargained it down to five times a day.

Islamic legend also identified an archetypal messenger bird, not the dove but the hoopoe, a more complex and assertive character. The crest of feathers on its head, which it can raise to look arrestingly like a crown, gave it an air of authority (its predilection for searching for cockroaches in dung heaps had to be ignored). In the mystic quest described in 'The Conference of the Birds' the hoopoe initiated and led the search for the truth about the simurgh,

Hoopoe, drawing by John White, 1585–93. British Museum.

earning it that disputed role of the king of the birds. Above all the hoopoe was associated with King Solomon, who had asked God for wisdom above power and wealth, and had been enabled to understand the language of birds, whom he consulted for esoteric information (a rare gift, but attributed to superhuman figures in many cultures). When Solomon, accompanied by angels and jinns (another form of winged spirit), ordered a muster of the birds, he was disturbed to find the hoopoe missing, but just as he was threatening to punish the delinquent bird a very bedraggled hoopoe flew in, not having eaten or drunk for three months, with news of a land of extraordinary wealth. Silver was as prevalent as dung in the markets and it was ruled by a woman, the Queen of Sheba. Naturally Solomon's mind turned to conquest, so he tied a letter to the hoopoe's wing and all the birds flew off together. They arrived as the sun was rising and the Queen was about to pray. Their beating wings blocked out the light and she was greatly disturbed, recognising calamity. Solomon's letter summoned the Queen of Sheba to pay homage or face invasion, so she departed bearing gifts but determined to test the wisdom of Solomon to the limit. There are some versions of the story that link the hoopoe (and Sheba) with water. A voluptuous Persian scene shows Sheba lying by a flowing stream with flowers and refreshments, communing with the hoopoe; and another version states that the original absence of the hoopoe infuriated Solomon because it caused 'a lack of water to perform the ablutions before prayer'. In some parts of Africa and Asia the seasonal movements of hoopoes are in response to rain, since they are searching for insects and frogs, and a drought might, in a confusion of cause and effect, have been attributed to their absence. By contrast, in more northerly climes, the hoopoe is a summer visitor. In England it appears only in warm dry summers likely to provide enough grasshoppers. It was presumably during such a sixteenth-century summer that John White painted this rare visitor.

Woodpeckers are more widely associated with rain than hoopoes (though they are natural allies, since hoopoes often nest in old woodpecker holes). Generally it was the tapping sound made by the woodpecker's beak against a tree

The Queen of Sheba reclines beside
a stream holding a love letter that the
hoopoe, perched in a bush at her feet,
will deliver to Solomon. Painting, Iran,
c.1590–1600. British Museum.

that was regarded as sympathetic rain magic. In ancient Greece a woodpecker tapping dance was performed and in Africa certain tribes beat a woodpecker drum for their rain dances. Audubon recorded an American Indian story of a woodpecker ending a drought by pecking at the tree where all the water was hidden until at last it gushed out and filled the creeks. According to another Native American tradition the woodpecker was connected to the heartbeat of the earth itself and its drumming had mystic connotations. Perhaps a similar thought inspired the Romans to link woodpeckers with the god of war Mars, who was originally a fertility god and therefore responsible for rainfall. His oracle was a woodpecker on a wooden column where auguries were given. In France it was believed that the green woodpecker was looking up at the clouds and crying 'pluie, pluie'; and in England, where the 'yaffle' sound was likened to laughing, it was said to call more before rain. The seventeenth-century antiquarian John Aubrey wrote, 'to this day the country people do divine of rain by their cry', although probably the sound simply carries further in the atmospheric conditions before rainfall. Woodpeckers are wondrous birds even without magic, amazingly adapted to their compulsive tapping. First their vertical position against a tree trunk is maintained by strong claws and stiff tail feathers, which fan out for balance. Their brains and eyes are fortified against the intense pressure of their hammering, and the chisel-like tips of their bills are actually sharpened by their pecking action against wood. Finally the purpose of all this is achieved when their long sticky tongues (complete with bristles) grab and extract insects from deep inside a tree.

The reactions of birds to changes of climate and season are among the world's great phenomena, often predictable but always astonishing: migration above all. If the arctic tern

European green woodpecker from
The Natural History of British Birds
by Edward Donovan, 1794–1815.

OPPOSITE: Arctic tern from
The Birds of America by
John James Audubon, 1827–38.

Drawn from Nature by J.J. Audubon. F.R.S. F.L.S.

Engraved, Printed, & Coloured by R. Havell. London. 1835.

Arctic Tern.
STERNA ARCTICA.

excels all others in flying annually from pole to pole, the movements of great flocks of birds between their northerly (or extreme southerly) summer breeding grounds and their less freezing winter homelands remains a source of wonder, and inspired a wealth of folklore before it was scientifically examined. Migrating birds are of course mainly seeking food resources, and their great V formations in the sky are instinctively designed to save energy (by up to fifty per cent) as each bird takes advantage of the wing-tip vortex of the bird in front to reduce drag. But to our ancestors it was otherworldly and the birds' migratory cries caused awe and speculation. Mysterious above all were the large water birds that could move through the elements of air, earth and water; the feathers that kept them airborne remained dry and pristine when they swam underwater or dabbled in mud. In Hindu mythology this represented the perfect balance that a soul might achieve – *hamsa* could be the meditative breathing of yoga, the flight of the swan or goose, or the bird on which a god or goddess descended to earth. From China to Scandinavia geese have been regarded as messengers between heaven and earth. In British folklore wild geese in flight were called Gabriel hounds, a ghostly pack of wild hunters baying across the sky as they conducted souls to the other world, as in the Scottish ballad: 'Grey goose and gander/Waft your wings together/And carry the good king's daughter/Over the one-strand river.' The one-strand river ('The undiscover'd country from whose bourn/No traveller returns') certainly signified death; although in this ballad the 'daughter' may originally have read 'banner' (a better rhyme), being a lament for the defeat of the Scots army at Flodden (in 1513) and

OPPOSITE: Earl Mar's daughter, illustration by Arthur Rackham from *Some British Ballads*, 1919.

the death of James IV on the battlefield, leaving his royal banner and his soul to be carried away on the wings of the wild geese. There were ballads in which the king's daughters were carried away, or fetched, but the most sinister was the tale of Earl Mar's daughter who on the eve of her wedding was snatched away by her bird-lover with a train of seven swans and twenty-four storks, leaving the wedding company powerless: 'but they saw a flock of pretty birds, that took their bride away'. In the Finnish *Kalevala*, a nineteenth-century epic derived from oral folklore, the swan of Tuonela – the land of the dead – floats majestically on the surrounding waters of the Tuoni river. When the hero Lemminkainan seeks an unattainable bride he is answered: 'When for me the swan thou killest, in the river of Tuoni, swimming in the death-black river, in the sacred stream and whirlpool. Thou canst try one crossbow only, but one arrow from thy quiver.' In Germanic legend Lohengrin, the knight of the swan, was a mysterious rescuer in a swan boat who could defend a maiden, even live happily with her, provided he was never asked his name.

These uncanny fragments may be survivals from the oldest bird lore of all, which is expressed for us in a few cave paintings and Ice Age carvings: the flying swan pendants from a site near Lake Baikal in Eastern Siberia, the heartland of bird migration; the tiny carving of a water bird, which may be a diver or cormorant, from the Hohlefels caves in Germany; and the oldest flutes, made from the hollow bones of swans and vultures. Prehistoric cave and rock paintings, teeming with animals and occasional birds, may have been simply expressing the surrounding world in an aesthetically pleasing way, but many further explanations have been suggested – that the dots which so frequently appear are patterns that the brain transmits during stages of hallucination, or that the hand-prints are markers pointing towards a sacred space – and some cave paintings do clearly depict shamanistic practices. At Hohlefels there is a lion-headed man and in the Lascaux caves a man with a bird's head and next to him a bird on a stick. Most striking is the New Zealand Maori bird-man with outspread, feathery

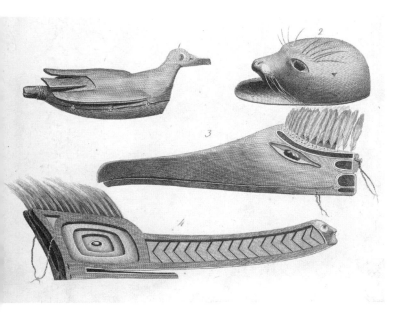

wings with smaller birds perched along them, from Te Waipounamu or South Island. (Maori people, believing birds carry messages between humans and gods, also made kites in the form of birds and flew them as a sacred ritual accompanied by chanting.) The rock-painted bird figures may represent a primitive form of those heroes and seers – such as Solomon, Taliesin and Siegfried – for whom it was claimed that they understood the language of birds. A shaman, in order to borrow mystic powers from wild animals or birds, had first to enter into a self-imposed hypnotic trance with the aid of fasting, dancing, drumming, chanting or hallucinogens. The purpose of undertaking such a dangerous experience, always on behalf of the community, could be to remove a threat, solve a problem, inspire an action, heal the sick or pacify restless ancestral spirits. The shaman wore a costume of skins or feathers to represent his (sometimes her) spirit guide and carried a staff carved with its image. Thus prepared the shaman's spirit could overcome the normal constraints of the body and travel superhuman distances in search of otherworldly wisdom. What better than to assume the powers of migratory birds?

In Canada and Siberia divers were the water birds most favoured in shamanistic practices. Carvings of divers were placed on tall posts (like the woodpeckers in ancient Rome). Shamans also wore pendants in the shape of divers and imitated their falsetto cries during the performance of their rituals. In ancient burial grounds in Alaska skulls were found inset with ivory eyes next to the skeletons of divers with similar eye plugs; as far away as the Faroe Islands lurked the belief that divers accompanied departed souls to the next world. Here too was a link with rain – in Shetland red-throated divers were known as 'rain geese' and in Norway they were said to foretell storms by their calls. A sense of a shaman's stages of suffering and final exultation is vividly expressed in the Anglo Saxon poem 'The Seafarer' from the tenth-century collection the *Exeter Book*. During this solitary journey into the extremity of the elements there was again the link with birds:

ABOVE: A bird decoy and two bird masks from Nootka Sound on the Pacific west coast of Canada. Drawing by John Webber, 1768–80.

OPPOSITE: Great Northern diver from *The Birds of America* by John James Audubon, 1827–38.

Native American medicine man,
'The flyer', in a dancing posture, drawing
by John White, 1585–93. British Museum.

I dwelt for a winter in the paths of exile, bereft of friendly kinsmen, hung about with icicles. Hail flew in showers, there I heard nothing but the roaring sea, the ice-cold wave. At those times the swan's song was my pleasure, the gannet's noise and the voice of the curlew instead of the laughter of men, the singing gull instead of the drinking of mead. Storms there beat the stony cliffs where the tern cried out, icy feathered.

The poem starts with a dread of the sea's perils and ends in triumph with a Christianised spiritual affirmation, but at its heart is the shaman's journey: 'And now my spirit twists out of my breast, my spirit out on the waterways over the whale's path. It soars widely through all the corners of the world. It comes back to me eager and unsated.'

When John White sketched the activities of the Algonquian Indians, whom he encountered on the Elizabethan expedition to North America, he included a shaman, who wore a bird above his ear as a sign of his calling and a pouch on his belt containing herbs and powders, including strong tobacco. (American shamans ingested tobacco in enormous quantities to induce an ecstatic trance.) The pose of White's Indian shaman, inscribed 'The flyer', may have been captured by White, deliberately or unconsciously, to echo that of Hermes (a popular emblematic figure in the Renaissance). Hermes was the Greek god, a trickster and shape-shifter, who guided souls to the underworld. He wore feathers on his cap and heels, and he too carried a pouch of herbs. Such attributes as feathered headdresses and cloaks, along with bird legends and superstitions, fairy tales of humans transformed into birds (including Ovid's *Metamorphoses*), and the recurring idea that eagles or cranes carry smaller birds on their backs (as the rock-painted Maori bird figure held birds along its wings) fall into context as remnants and memories of shamanistic practices, once considered vital to the survival of communities living on the edge of nature's vagaries and hardships.

Sunda wrinkled hornbill, drawing
from Indonesia, c.1818–1830.

Many birds in their courtship rituals act as if they were dancing, spreading their tails, stamping their feet, fluttering their wings, arching their necks, leaping and uttering all kinds of sounds from fierce cries to lovely melodies – all excellent inspiration for a tribe circling and drumming around their shaman to induce him into a trance. The circle is the natural, age-old form of both the watchers and the dance itself, even the heavenly dance of the angels. Of all the birds that have inspired human dances, the hornbill is one of the most sensational, and the dances are as widespread as the bird is indigenous – from northern India to South East Asia and Central Africa. The hornbill is named for its monstrous beak, curved downwards but reminiscent of a cow's horn (the first two vertebrae in the bird's neck are fused together to support its great weight). This asset is used not only for feeding but for fighting and display, its splendour emphasised by bright-coloured flesh and wattles and a casque on the upper beak which is eye-catching in shape and colour. In some species the casque is hollow and has holes, which act as a resonator for its calls. In the helmeted hornbill it is not hollow and the bird uses it as a battering ram in dramatic aerial jousts, a performance of which the great hornbill is also capable. In parts of central and western Africa, rather than simply imitating the movements and calls of the bird, fantastic replicas of its beaked head are carved and worn as dance costumes atop conical straw outfits or wooden frames draped in cloth.

Sometimes the beaks are hinged to clap open and shut and squawk, or supported on a pole in order to rotate from side to side. Such ritual dances were performed in the belief that the hornbill carried the souls of the dead to the underworld.

In some versions of Hindu myth the Garuda bird is a hornbill, though more generally he is part eagle, part man. In countless Indian miniatures Garuda appears high against the sky bearing the god Vishnu with his consort Lakshmi, often on rescue missions, since Garuda's attribute is to fight evil (especially in the form of serpents), like the Archangel Michael. When at rest he perches atop a pillar on Vishnu's palace. In Buddhist tales Garuda's wings created hurricanes and he could transform between bird and human shape, appear or disappear, become large or small. Indeed Garuda could be large enough for a man to hide in his feathers. In China the *peng* bird of Taoist legend had similar attributes, *peng* being the suffix for greatness. Garuda was a master of elixirs and enlightenment, just as all shamans had to know the secrets of herbs and healing; and medicinal superstitions lingered around certain birds. The eagle stone, for instance, extracted from among the eggs in an eagle's nest (at some peril to the finder, assuming the location was authentic) was much sought after to alleviate the pains and dangers of childbirth. As late as 1665 the German physician Johann Lorenz Bausch wrote a tract full of engravings of eagle stones, examining the most efficacious methods of application.

OPPOSITE: Vishnu flying on Garuda to rescue the elephant king. Drawing ascribed to Mihr Chand, c.1790.

CHAPTER FIVE

Birds of Ill Omen

Of all the birds whose behaviour has struck humans as unlucky, crows are the most foreboding, and ravens – being the largest of the crow family – even more so. 'The sad presaging raven,' wrote Christopher Marlowe '… in the shadow of the silent night, doth shake contagion from her sable wings' (*Jew of Malta*, 2.i). Their blackness contributed much to their sinister image, with the watchful eyes, and the patch of bristly feathers over the cruel beak. The way crows move distinguishes them too, as if they expect to inspire fear rather than feel it: the deliberate walk, the heavy lifting of the wings, and that particular rhythm of flapping and gliding overhead. The peremptory harshness of their call was acknowledged by Lady Macbeth: 'the raven himself is hoarse that croaks the fatal entrance of Duncan under my battlements' (*Macbeth*, 1.v).

Their reputation was justly earned, since they are carrion birds and in the past they haunted battlefields. Being very intelligent, crows knew well in advance what advancing armies presaged and therefore behaved like auguries: 'crows and kites fly o'er our heads … their shadows seem a canopy most fatal, under which our army lies ready to give up the ghost,' warns Cassius in the last act of *Julius Caesar*. Their natural but horrible expectation of the feast to come could not fail to rouse an echoing human response, and for such a thrill of aversion nothing, not even Shakespeare, could equal the Scottish ballad 'The Twa Corbies':

> As I was walking all alone,
> I heard twa corbies making a moan,
> The one unto the other say,
> 'Where shall we gang and dine today?'
>
> 'In behind yon auld fail dyke,
> I wot there lies a new slain knight;
> And nobody kens that he lies there,
> But his hawk, his hound and his lady fair.
>
> …

> Many a one for him makes moan,
> But none shall ken where he is gone,
> O'er his white bones, when they are bare,
> The wind shall blow for evermair.'

Such macabre imaginings were also characterised in an ironic medieval tale called 'The Three Living and the Three Dead' (see p. 90), in which a group of carousing youths met their equivalent number of skeletons. The theme was echoed in German wall paintings of the Dance of Death, in Chaucer's *Pardoner's Tale*, and in this drollery from the border of a Dutch *Book of Hours*, made in Maastricht around 1300. It was meant as an exemplary reminder to stick to the straight and narrow, and for good measure a crow hopefully watches the doom-laden encounter. Other drolleries in medieval religious manuscripts, accompanying the popular scene of Noah's Ark, provided the clue which the Bible does not mention as to why the raven did not return to the Ark. Once the waters receded there was plenty of carrion on which it could feed and Noah, realising this, released the raven first. The Islamic version of the flood story does not feature the raven and the dove in black and white as the Bible does, but acknowledges their separate roles.

The intelligence of ravens and crows in pursuit of food (modern science has tested their use of tools and timers with impressive results) causes them to pursue carnivorous beasts and huntsmen (they may even help to find the prey) and also makes them infallible land birds. When freed from a ship (Noah's Ark again) they promptly head for the nearest land, which they can probably spot at 90 miles (145 km) away. Norse navigators may have used ravens thus, releasing them to detect the direction of a new landmass such as Iceland, the British Isles and even America. Incidentally ravens were held

OPPOSITE: 'The Twa Corbies', illustration by Arthur Rackham, from *Some British Ballads*, 1919.

'The Three Living and the Three Dead',
from the *Maastricht Hours*, early 14th century.

in awe by the original Native American tribes, figuring in great carvings on totem poles and the prows of canoes and inspiring many tales of magic and trickery as well as creation myths. Ravens were certainly important to the Old Norse gods. Odin had two, named Thought and Memory, who acted as his messengers and spies, augmenting his wisdom. When Odin hung for nine days on the tree of knowledge they sustained him (as they also sustained Elijah in the wilderness and various desert fathers). Such concepts derived from observing the tireless efforts of parent crows in feeding their own demanding, noisy nestlings. The Valkyries of Norse mythology were terrifying female battle gods and shape-shifters who took the form of crows. In the Icelandic *Njal's Saga* the Valkyries themselves were weavers, creating a spear-grey fabric patterned in blood, with arrows for shuttles. Their Celtic counterpart was the Morrigan, goddess of sovereignty as well as battle, the Washer at the Ford, who before a battle would appear in the shallows of a river washing the bloodstained clothes of those about to die. During the battle she hovered over the action in the form of a raven, spreading dread or encouragement according to allegiance. But the Morrigan could also shape-shift into a great beauty, and it was because the Irish hero Cuchulain rejected her advances that he was doomed to die in battle. The Celtic strands of Arthurian legend, especially relating to King Arthur's half-sister Morgana and the Grail King in Castle Corbenic (Raven Castle), retained this supernatural sense of the raven's powers – and from the unlikely source of Miguel Cervantes' *Don Quixote* came this unexpected claim: 'Have you not read sir, the famous exploits of King Arthur, of whom there goes an old tradition that this king did not die but that by magic art he was turned into a raven and that he shall reign again?' The Welsh hero Bran (the name means 'raven') survived death in the form of a prophetic head, which his followers finally brought to London and buried where the Tower of London now stands – hence the necessary presence of ravens.

Elijah and the raven from Mandeville's *Travels*, early 15th century.

The Raven of ill-omen

Fr.

'The Raven of ill-omen', illustration by
Stephen Reid from *Cuchulain,
the Hound of Ulster* by Eleanor Hull, 1909.

Over the centuries these dark birds have inhabited a vast hinterland of myth and fancy into which Edgar Allen Poe could delve for his 1845 poem 'The Raven': that 'grim, ungainly, ghastly, gaunt and ominous bird of yore' that kept tapping 'something louder than before'; until it gained entrance, 'with many a flirt and flutter' and 'perched upon a bust of Pallas just above my chamber door':

> Ghastly, grim and ancient Raven wandering from
>   the Nightly Shore,
> Tell me what thy lordly name is on the Night's
>   Plutonian shore,
> Quoth the Raven 'Nevermore'.

Other members of the crow family are less sinister. Rooks are the noisy sociable ones with their colonies of nests; jackdaws the little ones with amusing aerial dives; choughs live by the seaside; and jays are shy woodland beauties with coloured feathers. But magpies are the real characters, and also beautiful with their dramatic black and white contrasts, the sudden sheen of deep blue and green as they spread their wings and tails, and that long-tailed flight pattern. In Australia the black and white areas are reversed and in certain American and Asian magpies the blue and green feathers predominate. The 'pie' in their name is shortened from pied but, since they share the carrion habits of other crows, the 'mag' (shortened from maggot) is the unpleasant part: 'Blood will have blood ... Augurs and understood relations have by maggot-pies and choughs and rooks brought forth the secret'st man of blood' (*Macbeth*, 3.iv). Their chattering, mocking, mimicking qualities made magpies the stuff of folklore and proverb, including the story that they lost their bright colours when they mocked Christ on the cross. But in Christian art magpies are more often found in Nativity scenes, including Piero della Francesca's, because at that moment all time stood still and all movement was stopped, even the restless magpie's; although in Pieter Bruegel's paintings the bird imagery is bitter and mocking, especially the 1568 *Magpie on the Gallows*.

'The Raven', illustration by
William Heath Robinson from
The Poems of Edgar Allan Poe, 1900.

Poets from Christopher Marlowe to Ted Hughes, seeking for dark imagery and not content with the colour of a crow's feathers, made it a creature of the night, but crows – though they fly at dusk – are not nocturnal. For this the owl is superbly adapted – and correspondingly spooky. The huge staring eyes, long-sighted and light-gathering, give it vision far greater than its prey and, because the eyes are fixed in their sockets to look straight forward, the head itself can rotate to look backwards (with several extra vertebrae to make the neck so flexible). The wide face with the conspicuous circle of feathers around each eye certainly magnifies their intensity, but has more to do with hearing, because these feathers funnel sound into the owl's ears, enabling it to detect and calculate the distance of its prey from the slightest rustling. The small downward-pointing beak also helps to direct sound into the ears and allows the maximum field of vision. By contrast the owl itself is silent in pursuit of its prey: its flight feathers have serrated edges and a velvety surface that together reduce wind resistance and muffle the slow wing-beats. Such stealth is augmented by the bird's dull mottled colours that render it almost invisible in dim light – until it gives an unearthly hoot or screech – the 'desolation of the owl' according to the Old Testament, or Keats' 'gloom-bird's hated screech'. In parts of Africa it is the bird with no name, simply 'the one that makes you afraid', because in virtually all cultures the owl's call has been considered a harbinger of death. Was it for that shudder of fear that an owl was engraved in the Chauvet caves in France about 30,000 years ago? Possibly it represented another shamanistic messenger to the otherworld, an ancestor of witchcraft.

In the Middle East owls have been particularly associated with caves and ancient walls. In Arabic the little owl is named 'mother of ruins', and the scops owl seen here has a similar reputation. The tufts of feathers that distinguish it, often called ears or horns, are possibly used by the birds for signalling to one another, but they certainly give them a listening air. This image (like the Night Journey of Muhammad) is taken from a copy of the *Khamsa* of Nizami

ABOVE: Little owl, drawing by Albrecht Dürer, 1508. Graphische Sammlung Albertina, Vienna.

OPPOSITE: Emperor Anushirvan hears owls remarking on the number of ruined villages in his kingdom from Nizami's *Khamsa*, 'Five Poems', Tabriz, 1539–43.

created for the Safavid Shah Tahmasp in sixteenth-century Iran. The ruins are the setting for the story of Nurshivan, a king who tended to forget the sufferings of his people in pursuit of his own glorious reputation. One day while out riding Nurshivan came to a deserted town and found two owls hooting to one another on a ruined palace wall. They were discussing the commercial value of derelict houses 'if our noble ruler continues in his present course' – a subtle example of how the symbolism of owls combines foreboding with wisdom. Soon after the *Khamsa* was completed Shah Tahmasp abandoned his artistic patronage and his artists dispersed. However, the link between owls and ruins was manifest centuries later during the First World War, when rats and mice swarmed into the fighting lines followed by barn owls, who had a plenitude of ruined houses to nest in and desolation in unlimited quantity.

The nightjar, in its smaller, gentler way, bears much the same folkloric odium as the owl, although references to it are more rarefied. Lord Ferdinand de Rothschild, who founded the great house Waddeston Manor in 1877, feared for its future, imagining the collections dispersed, the terraces crumbling and 'the melancholy cry of the nightjar sounding from the deserted towers'. This bird too flies silently in the dark with huge, night-vision eyes and camouflaging grey-brown plumage, so that its disembodied song 'whip poor will' inspires superstitious dread. A long-held conviction that it stole milk from the teats of goats and cows earned it the name goat-sucker (even in Latin) and it was also believed to infect cattle with a parasitic disease. This was the kind of prejudice Gilbert White, the eighteenth-century naturalist and curate at Selborne in Hampshire, wished he could dispel: 'the least observation and attention would convince men that these birds injure neither the goatherd nor the grazier but that they are perfectly harmless and subsist only, being night birds, on night insects'. In America Audubon also developed a protective fondness for nightjars, especially *Caprimulgus carolinensis* with their variant call:

About the middle of March the forests of Louisiana are heard to echo with the well-known notes of this interesting bird. No sooner has the sun disappeared and the nocturnal insects emerged than the sounds 'chuck wills widow', repeated with great clearness and power six or seven times in as many seconds, strike the ear, bringing to mind a pleasure mingled with melancholy which I have often found very soothing.

When alarmed, nightjars ruffle all their feathers, open their enormous bristly beaks (designed to trap insects) very wide indeed and hiss much like a snake, the creature to which they have the deepest aversion. It was in this repellent pose that Audubon chose to portray his nightjars.

Whereas the superstitions attaching to crows, owls and other birds of darkness and night are explicable and virtually universal, the proverbial reputation of the albatross is based almost entirely on one poem, Samuel Taylor Coleridge's 'The Rime of the Ancient Mariner' (although the poet himself had many sources of inspiration, including laudanum). At the time the idea was born, Coleridge and William Wordsworth were together in the West Country, agonising over their writings, and Coleridge was seeking a theme that would reflect his own struggles with guilt. It was Wordsworth who was reading George Shelvocke's account of a circumnavigation undertaken between 1719 and 1722, in which was described 'the largest sort of sea-fowls extending their wings twelve or thirteen feet and called albitroses'. Shelvocke's ship ran into the terrifying storms that characterise Cape Horn, during which a black albatross 'accompanied us for several days, hovering about us as if he had lost himself'. The crew imagined it to be a bird of ill omen, linked to the 'continued

OPPOSITE: Chuckwills Widow (nightjar) from *The Birds of America* by John James Audubon, 1827–38.

PLATE 16.

Chuck-wills Widow,

CAPRIMULGUS CAROLINENSIS, Bris.

Male.1.Female.2.

Harlequin Snake.

Drawn from Nature, and Published by John J. Audubon. F.R.S.E.L.S. Engraved, Printed, & Coloured by R. Havell.

series of contrary tempestuous winds which had oppressed us ever since we had got into this sea'. One of the crew shot the albatross, 'not doubting we should have a fair wind after it', but instead the winds grew so severe that it took six weeks to sight the coast of Chile. The South American Indians living near the coasts haunted by these enormous birds had their own superstitions, including this legend – an albatross flapping its wings on a certain promontory jutting out into the sea caused a persistent stormy wind until the bird was captured. Then the air grew so calm and still that scum covered the sea and it stank (a phenomenon described by Coleridge). The people were just as troubled by this as by the storm, so they agreed to release the bird on condition that it beat its wings gently. Other tribes had similar beliefs about the powers of the albatross and held ceremonies of propitiation with dance masks made from albatross feathers, but Indian legends made no mention of killing the albatross.

When in Coleridge's poem the Ancient Mariner committed his apparently pointless crime, the ship had been blown by a storm towards the South Pole, into a sea of ice, and it was then, through the snow fog, that there suddenly appeared a great seabird that landed on the deck, as they do. But an albatross cannot take off again from a ship's deck, so it remained and the crew fed and petted it. The ice began to split and a wind sprang up from the south enabling the ship to continue its journey northwards. Then the Mariner shot the albatross: 'And I had done a hellish thing/And it would work 'em woe/For all averred I had killed the bird/That made the breeze to blow.' However in the first version of the poem there were lines (which Coleridge later omitted) that proved the albatross was shot for food. The storm had

OPPOSITE: The shooting of the albatross, illustration by Gustav Doré from 'The Rime of the Ancient Mariner' by Samuel Taylor Coleridge, 1877.

lasted weeks (like Shelvocke's), 'for days and weeks it played us freaks', and when the crew shared their food with the albatross it was not from any surplus: 'the mariners fed it biscuit worms'. During the eighteenth century ill-nourished crews on long sea voyages had become accustomed to eating albatross. On Captain Cook's voyages the ship's naturalists all mentioned this: Joseph Banks on the *Endeavour* noted that 'the men eat heartily of them'; Reinhold Foster on the second voyage in 1772 wrote, 'we found them to be extremely curious but they paid with their lives for this curiosity'; and his son George Foster noted, 'they skim always on the surface of the sea and afford a good palatable food'. Captain Cook himself found a meal of albatross 'exceedingly good'. Besides this, the crew could make pipes from the long hollow wing bones, tobacco pouches from the big webbed feet and warm slippers from the downy skins. In 1916 when drifting Antarctic sea ice had crushed Shackleton's *Endurance* the flesh of albatross kept the shipwrecked sailors alive. After a desperate, gale-tossed 800-mile (1,290-km) journey their lifeboat reached South Georgia Island and 'there we found the nests of albatrosses, the nestlings were fat and lusty ... what a stew it was, the flesh was white and succulent and the bones not fully formed almost melted in our mouths'. No sense of sin there. But Coleridge's own sense of sin was highly developed and, since he opposed slavery, it no doubt extended to an awareness of the ruthless society he lived in, exploiting other races and the natural world in the endless process of expansion. Three hundred years earlier Columbus himself, returning to Europe in the first triumph of discovery, lamented that the Caribbeans were so innocent, unsuspicious and doomed.

'The Rime of the Ancient Mariner' is too mysterious to be precisely didactic, and the action is set in a time before Magellan rounded Cape Horn: 'we were the first that ever burst into that silent sea'. The Mariner used a crossbow to shoot the albatross, a medieval detail which fitted Coleridge's aura of superstitious dread and fear of sin. There was, however, a European fancy that seagulls were the souls of drowned sailors, perhaps on account of their unearthly call, and

Wandering albatross from
The Birds of Australia
by John Gould, 1848–69.

albatrosses were sometimes said to be ships' captains who had perished passing the Cape. Herman Melville in *Moby Dick* described a captured albatross and gave full weight to its supernatural air:

> I remember the first albatross I ever saw. It was during a prolonged gale in waters hard upon the Antarctic seas ... a regal thing of unspotted whiteness, at intervals it arched its vast archangel wings ... it uttered cries, as some king's ghost in supernatural distress. Through its inexpressible, strange eyes methought I peeped to secrets which took hold of God.

Before the rest of the crew on the Ancient Mariner's ship dropped dead, cursing him, they hung the albatross around his neck as a punishment which became proverbial, and which clinched the bird's ominous reputation.

Naturally, given its name, the albatross is generally pictured as ghostly white (as Gustav Doré did in his atmospheric illustrations) but some, including Bruce Chatwin in *In Patagonia*, have cast doubt on the possibility of hanging so huge a bird round anyone's neck and suggested

that Coleridge intended the sooty albatross, which is smaller, and which would correspond with Shelvocke's account. Perhaps John Gould should have the last word, describing the albatrosses he saw while living in Australia:

> There is also a widespread sooty albatross, the only species that flies directly over a ship, which it frequently does in blowing weather, poising itself over the mast head, offering so inviting a mark for a gunner that it often forfeits its life, and if it is shot a little to windward it is almost certain to fall on board.

However the white, black-browed albatross is the most common in the Southern Ocean, known to every voyager that has rounded either of the Capes, equally numerous in the Atlantic and Pacific Oceans. In a storm its snowy white contrasts with the murky clouds. This species is the most fearless of man and approaches close to vessels. When taken on deck, from which it cannot take wing, it becomes readily tame. The birds follow vessels for hundreds of miles and no doubt they circle the globe with their great powers of flight.

CHAPTER SIX

Symbol and Metaphor

During the fifteenth century, manuscript decoration paid increasing attention to realistic details from the natural world, including birds, and when they appeared all around a page some at least may have offered a message to decipher. In this Annunciation from a fifteenth-century French *Book of Hours*, the dove of the Holy Spirit descends from God to the Virgin in a ray of light, the angel Gabriel kneels in a tiny columned alcove of this wonderful confection of medieval architecture, and three Old Testament prophets lean out from balconies to unfurl their scrolls of prophesies. Above the Virgin hangs a caged bird, symbol of her virginity. By contrast the birds in the margin are free, and probably singing in jubilant praise at this miraculous conception. They include wrens, hoopoes, a robin, a bullfinch and a goldfinch, a pheasant and a snipe, a parrot, a woodpecker and a kingfisher, a wading bird and what birdwatchers call a 'small brown job'. There is nothing unusual, but unique to this manuscript are the mating sparrows in the margin directly behind the Virgin. Either this is a humorous glance at the way reproduction normally takes place or it represents sex as sin. Sparrows were regarded as lecherous little creatures (Chaucer called them 'the sparwe, Venus' son') and because of their cheeky familiarity they represented the common and vulgar. In 1559 a Lutheran pastor in Dresden sought to exterminate the sparrows because of their 'incessant and extremely vexatious chattering and scandalous acts of unchastity committed during the service to the hindrance of God's word'.

However, sparrows were mentioned affectionately in two of the gospels. Matthew 10.29 states, 'Are not two sparrows sold for a farthing, and not one of them shall fall without the knowledge of your Father which is in heaven'; or as Shakespeare put it, 'There is a special providence in the fall of a sparrow' (*Hamlet*, 5.ii). In his eighth-century *Ecclesiastical History of the English People* the Venerable Bede conjured a moving image:

The present life of man, oh King, seems to me like the swift flight of a sparrow through the room where you

ABOVE: Male sparrow from the *Sherborne Missal*, c.1399–1407.

OPPOSITE: The Annunciation from the London *Hours*, c.1407.

sit at supper in winter, with your commanders and ministers and a good fire in the midst, while storms of wind and rain and snow prevail outside. The sparrow while he is within is safe but he immediately vanishes out of sight into the dark winter from which he emerged.

The Roman poet Catullus (d. 54 BC) wrote an ode to a pet sparrow, 'my sweet girl's delight', which was famous during the centuries when Latin was read for pleasure, and received a fresh injection of popularity when it went to an early printing press in 1472. The Latin captured the tweeting of the sparrow 'cui primum digitum dare appetenti', and the innuendo was delicate. (In an English translation, 'to whose greedy attack she gives her fingertip', all this is lost.) Alas the sparrow died but its quaintly libidinous reputation lived on.

If any bird could soar like the righteous soul straight up towards heaven it was the skylark (Shelley's 'blithe spirit'), singing as it rose. Twice Shakespeare wrote 'the lark at heaven's gate sings' (though this was in the context of earthly love), but the manuscript illuminators had got there first. The artist who painted birds in the borders of the *Sherborne Missal* linked the skylark with a vignette representing Christ's Ascension into heaven, simply showing his feet leaving the ground in a shower of light; while a celestial blue vision in a French *Book of Hours* features a tiny lark high up at heaven's gate. Around God and Jesus the angels circle in their ranks above the green globe of the world, the white dove descends, and in the border below a parrot is flying that is green like the world.

The goldfinch from the *Sherborne Missal*, like the lark, had a symbolic meaning relating it to the accompanying

The Trinity from a French *Book of Hours*, mid-15th century.

OPPOSITE: Goldfinch from the *Sherborne Missal*, c.1399–1407.

image. This colourful bird became the darling of over 200 Renaissance artists (including Raphael, Leonardo da Vinci and Albrecht Dürer) who painted the childhood of Christ and included a goldfinch as a symbol of the crucifixion. The splash of red on its head linked it with the redeeming blood of Christ and its fondness for thistledown and teasels was a reminder of the crown of thorns – some legends even suggested the goldfinch (or the robin or swallow) tried to remove the thorns and earned red feathers as an enduring mark of sanctity. In Piero della Francesca's *The Nativity* (1470–5) a goldfinch is perched on a thistle-head. But in the *Sherborne Missal* attention is being drawn mainly to the gold (which the goldfinch uses for display in courtship rituals). In the vignette above the goldfinch the three kings are bringing their golden gifts, and above them in the star the tiny child appears. The poor goldfinch had a fateful combination of colourful plumage and sweet twittering song (imitated by the flute in Vivaldi's concerto *Il Gardellino*), which made it popular as a caged bird. Thomas Hardy found a caged goldfinch particularly poignant: 'Within a churchyard on a recent grave/I saw a little cage/That jailed a goldfinch. All was silence save/Its hops from stage to stage'. Hardy used the image again in his novel of ill-fated relationships *The Mayor of Casterbridge*, in which the bird was given as a wedding present, but forgotten, and left to starve under a bush outside.

In books, paintings and manuscripts birds are usually mere details, but they can be very meaningful in their context, like a jewel in its setting. Similarly one phrase snatched from a poem may transcend all the rest. Memorable instances include: George Meredith's lark ascending, 'he drops the silver chain of sound'; Gerard Manley Hopkins, 'as kingfishers catch fire'; T. S. Eliot in a garden of lost memories following 'the deception of the thrush'; even Andrew Motion describing a sparrow as 'piebald shitter'; and certainly Ted Hughes' swallow 'twinkling away over the lake', 'setting her tail to harpoon a wind', 'snipping midges' and above all her plumage: 'Sahara clay ovens at mirage heat glazed her blues'. Swallows more than any other birds, and almost universally, have been harbingers of spring – creating

Barn Swallow
HIRUNDO AMERICANA.
Male 1. Female 2.

Drawn from Nature by J.J.Audubon FRS. FLS.   Engraved, Printed & Coloured, by R.Havell, 1833.

rejoicing when the first swallow was sighted. In Cornwall the moment was greeted by jumping in the air, in Russia songs were composed and in parts of Germany a watchman waited in a high tower to signal its arrival. In southern Africa swallows were believed to be the ancestors of the tribe returning to comfort the living. And from China to the igloos of the Inuit it was considered lucky to have swallows nesting nearby. Of course those who study the matter can tell the difference between swallows, swifts and martins but 'swallow' tends to be the generic name for the birds whose migrations seemed more mysterious than any other, whose nest-building habits were equally intriguing, and who seemed perpetually airborne – 'swifts copulate as they fly' wrote the eighteenth-century naturalist Gilbert White. Through his correspondence and notes White led the way in establishing observational studies and keener accuracy, and as he watched them congregating in flocks on the church tower at Selborne in Hampshire (where he was curate), hirundines (the name he gave to swallows, martins and swifts) remained one of his greatest puzzling delights. As a predecessor of Darwin, White also realised that closely related species diverged curiously in their propensities and the environmental conditions they accepted. For instance, if migration was prompted by food supplies, why would swifts leave in August, two months before swallows and martins? They make roughly comparable nests, either outside or inside buildings, whereas sand martins, the smallest of the hirundines, nest in sand cliffs into which they tunnel – 'perseverance will accomplish anything ...' wrote White. Meanwhile his revered contemporary Dr Johnson could still assure his audience that 'swallows certainly sleep all the winter. A number of them

conglobulate together by flying round and round and then all in a heap throw themselves under water and lie in the bed of a river'. Even the great eighteenth-century naturalist and taxonomer Carl Linnaeus seems to have subscribed to the theory of hibernation in riverine mud, and perhaps Christian symbolism added to the tenacious affection with which this view was held. Since swallows reappeared around Easter they represented the Resurrection of Christ, and if they rose from the earth the correspondence to rising from the grave was all the more perfect. (In the 1490s the Venetian artist Carlo Crivelli painted *The Madonna of the Swallow* with this symbolism in mind.) Gilbert White made his observations on migration versus hibernation from the 1760s onwards, corresponding earnestly with fellow scientists who claimed to have uncovered hibernating swallows, and searching for them himself. However his brother, John White, while stationed at Gibraltar wrote confirming that 'myriads of the swallow kind traverse the straits, south to north and back again, according to the season'.

When John Gould was researching the birds of Australia in the nineteenth century he saw the matter in reverse, as the birds arrived from far in the north to nest in southern Australia, arriving in August and departing in March. In that time the fairy martins raised two or three broods in their bottle-shaped nests, which they built under eaves and verandas just like house martins: 'they work together in small groups, one inside receives the mud, and eventually there can be 30 or 40 nests together pointing down or at right angles and all lined with feathers and fine grass'. For Audubon in America the barn swallow was the harbinger of spring, seldom appearing before the final melting of the snows, congregating in barns or under bridges, 'and proceeding to build their nests of river mud from the bottom up in regular layers, mixing a considerable quantity of long slender grasses which often dangle for several inches beneath the bottom of the nest'. Like many birds with powerful symbolic associations, swallows were adopted by healers of all sorts from tribal shamans to physicians and compilers of medical encyclopedias. Particularly legendary was the swallow stone

OPPOSITE: Barn swallow from
The Birds of America by
John James Audubon, 1827–38.

ABOVE: Fairy Martin from *The Birds of America* by John James Audubon, 1827–38.

OPPOSITE: Cuckoo from *The Natural History of British Birds* by Edward Donovan, 1794–1815.

or chelidonius, a semi-precious stone believed to be found in a swallow's nest (or inside a nestling), and sought as a cure for blindness.

There is of course another harbinger of spring, another migratory bird from Africa; it is in no way as appealing as the swallow except for its call: 'Summer is icumen in/Loud sing cuckoo/Groweth seed and bloweth mead/And springeth the wood now/Sing cuckoo' (Anon). It is indeed a magical and increasingly rare sound. Though all the sentimental nostalgia that William Wordsworth could summon will not quite extract the irony from his claim that 'the earth we pace/again appears to be/an unsubstantial faery place/That is fit home for thee'. Where do its nesting habits fit into that concept? While other birds are diligently and charmingly building their nests and rearing their young here comes the cuckoo, which lays its egg effortlessly, and when its gross young hatches it does its best to starve and murder its baby hosts. 'Our most hardened crooks', wrote W. H. Auden, 'are sincerely shocked by your nesting habits.' And there was the further suspicion that the delightful call, 'unpleasing to a married ear', signified a cuckold.

Few birds have retained their picturesque but archaic symbolism into the twenty-first century (except perhaps for use in poetic metaphors). One that has is the robin, star of many a cheap and cheerful Christmas card. The name means red, a colour that evokes warmth, as does the way the robin sings even in winter, and even at night, and is always there to inspect outdoor activities that might unearth worms and grubs. The robin's association with earth has always been strong, extending to folk beliefs relating to the burial of the dead, and a curious alliance with the wren who featured in midwinter rituals of death and burial. The rhyme 'Who killed cock robin' may date back to some such garbled belief; there is a fifteenth-century stained glass window in Buckland Abbey in Gloucestershire showing a robin shot by an arrow. The red breast could be imagined to represent blood rather than warmth and the refrain has the sound of a popular lament, 'all the birds of the air fell a sighing and a sobbing, when they heard of the death of poor cock robin'. Was there

a midwinter contest between two aggressive little birds, robin and sparrow or robin and wren? The first printed version of the rhyme appeared only in 1744, leading some to suggest it was a sardonic rhyme about the fall of Robert Walpole in 1742. It may have been reworked for this, but there are versions elsewhere in Europe, including Germany, and since the name robin (like Robert) is Germanic a far older origin is likely.

Blackbirds have inspired another baffling nonsense rhyme: 'Sing a song of sixpence/A pocket full of rye/Four and twenty blackbirds/Baked in a pie.' Both the phrase 'a song for sixpence' and the idea of baking live birds in a pie date back to Tudor times. An Italian cookbook produced in 1549 and translated into English in 1598 contained a recipe 'to make pies so that birds may be alive in them and fly out when it is cut up'. And in 1600 when Henri IV of France married Marie de' Medici the wedding feast began with a pie from which songbirds flew. There are other stories of novelties inside sixteenth-century pies. When the Abbot of Glastonbury hoped to avoid having his Abbey dissolved by Henry VIII he sent the king a pie in which, as a placatory gift, were hidden the deeds of twelve manorial estates belonging to the Abbey. Although there is no printed version of the nursery rhyme before the eighteenth century, an oral tradition still links it to Henry VIII's religious changes. The blackbirds could be Catholic monks, the king in his counting house could be Henry gloating over the proceeds of the Dissolution, the Queen eating bread and honey could be Catherine of Aragon, and Anne Boleyn the maid with her nose pecked off. Whatever the rhyme's meaning, many have mined it for satire, song lines and allusions, including Lord Byron, the Beatles, James Joyce, Virginia Woolf, Agatha Christie and W. B. Yeats, who said, 'you can refute Hegel but not the song of sixpence'. Poets tend to treat blackbirds as creatures of shadow and suggestion. Wallace Stevens wrote 'Thirteen ways of looking at a blackbird' including the lines: 'When the blackbird flew out of sight/It marked the edge of one of many circles'. In Glanmore, his Irish cottage, Seamus Heaney watched a blackbird 'cavorting through the yard ... a

wing bring

king sing

string

little stillness dancer'; and there was more stillness in Edward Thomas's pre-war memory of Adlestrop: 'And for that minute a blackbird sang/Close by, and round him, mistier/Farther and farther, all the birds/Of Oxfordshire and Gloucestershire'.

It is not surprising that chickens, the most widely domesticated of all birds, should have their own nonsense verse, which sounds as if it might be rude: 'Cock a doodle do/My dame has lost her shoe/My master's lost his fiddling stick/And doesn't know what to do.' But beyond the ridiculous rhyme (which does not seem to have attached itself to any particular historic figure) and the innuendo surrounding the word cock (traceable to Priapus, the Greek god of lust), impressive layers of history and symbolism unfold. All domestic poultry are descended from the red jungle fowl of central South East Asia (the area stretching from Burma to Indonesia). The ancestral male was large and fierce with red wattles and comb, spurs and the triumphant crowing call; the ancestral female was dun-coloured, brooded over her eggs and clucked. Subspecies and hybrids evolve very fast in chickens but among the huge variety of domestic breeds the DNA of the red jungle fowl is ever-present. First they were taken along the trade routes to China, Japan and beyond (the first fossil chicken bones come from northeast China and date from 5400 BC) and to India, which was the gateway to western Asia. By 2000 BC cuneiform tablets in Mesopotamia were referring to 'the bird of Meluhha' (probably the Indus Valley) and the astrologers of ancient Babylon identified the constellation we call Orion as the divine herald with his attendant bird the cock. In Egypt during the following millennium cockerels were painted in tombs, bred as fighting birds and an artificial method of incubating eggs was developed, thus freeing up hens to lay more. The Romans intensified these techniques in large organised farms, protected from predators, where chickens were fattened by diet and also by castrating cocks to create capons. However, by the time the Romans invaded Britain chickens were already there.

Scientific encyclopedists from Aristotle and Pliny to Ulisse Aldrovandi (the eminent sixteenth-century naturalist

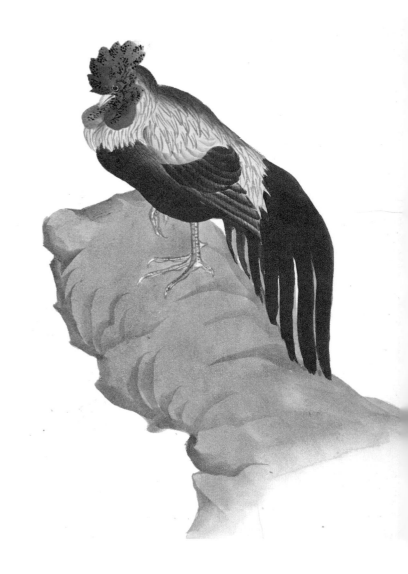

Cockerel from *Chorui Hiako Shiu*, an album of coloured drawings, Japan, c.1860–70.

based at the University of Bologna) puzzled over the origins of different types of chicken, fully aware that the area of diversity lay in the East and that some breeds were enormous, some lean and very aggressive, and some black right through to their flesh. In *Ornithologiae*, Aldrovandi included illustrations of the frizzle-headed fowl, an Indian rooster with no spurs, tail or crest, which he had received from the Grand Duke of Tuscany; also the 'wool bearing hen' found 'in civitate Quelinfu in regno Mangi'. This bird Aldrovandi took from 'a certain cosmographic map' (concealing his sources because, in those days of discovery, maps were state secrets) – in fact it was the Chinese who developed the breed now called the Silkie, which has feathers like silk or wool, a docile variety mentioned by Marco Polo who described it as 'furry'. The greatest mystery is how chickens first reached America. They too have the genes of the red jungle fowl and could possibly have passed into America with the first human arrivals about 10,000 years ago, or been brought across the Pacific to South America by Polynesian or Chinese travellers. When Magellan reached the coast of Brazil he 'picked up a great store of chickens ... for one fish hook, or a knife, they gave me six chickens'. The Spanish Conquistadors in Mexico found the Aztecs and Maya using chickens for divination; Pizarro on reaching the kingdom of the Incas found their leader Atahualpa named from a rooster (*hualpa*) and wearing feathered robes; the Colombian Indians developed their own unusual breed, the Araucana, which lays eggs with blue shells and seems to have been achieved by crossing chickens with pheasants.

Sacrifice and divination with cockerels became as universal as the birds themselves. The Romans even took chickens on their military campaigns and observed their appetite carefully before battles, regarding a rapid consumption of grain as an augury of victory. The fury with which cocks fight was considered an example to armies. Themistocles, an Athenian general in the fifth-century BC Persian wars, inspired his soldiers by pointing out the advantage of instinctive aggression: 'behold these do not fight for their gods, ancestors, glory, liberty or the safety

ABOVE: Woman feeding a hen and chicks from the *Luttrell Psalter*, c.1320–40.

BELOW: Frizzle-headed fowl from *Ornithologiae* by Ulisse Aldrovandi, 1599.

Japanese black fighting cock, *Chorui Hiako Shiu*, an album of coloured drawings, Japan, c.1860–70.

of their children, but only because one will not give way to the other'. A cockerel contrives a thrilling display of aggression. As a prelude he struts in a half-circle with one wing extended down, then both wings are spread wide and all the feathers puffed out. St Augustine (an unlikely source) thrilled to the narrative: 'their heads thrust forward, their combs inflated, they strike vigorously while evading each other. In every motion another higher reason guides them. Finally there is the proud song of the victor, his limbs drawn up with dominant scorn.' There is an Italian proverb 'the rooster jumps' to signify fighting spirit, because they fight with their spurs, and humans have supplemented this natural endowment with an arsenal of sharp metal strapped to the birds' legs. Cockfighting is still widespread in Latin America, South East Asia and India. As recently as 2011 there was a ruling in the Madras high court to permit a cockfight because 'the villagers' religious sentiments would be hurt if the cockfight was not allowed'. In both Hindu and Buddhist practices cockfighting has been an integral part of funerals and propitiation rituals. The excitement is undeniable and, given a strong primitive belief, it has been interpreted as summoning the spirits as a prelude to sacrifice. The artist Johann Zoffany (who spent six years painting in India when he fell out of favour at George III's court) captured the degradation and fascination of cockfighting as a blood sport in *Colonel Mordaunt's Cock Match*. The cockfight took place in Lucknow in 1784. The Nawab of Oudh, a debauched individual, stands in the centre of the painting gesturing towards Mordaunt (all in white) who had brought European game cocks to pit against the Indian breeds. The outcome is not recorded, but even the Governor General Warren Hastings was present, and although he declined to be represented it was he who commissioned the painting.

Although the aggression of cockerels was paramount, their crowing at daybreak was more symbolic. The Roman poets liked it: Ovid called it 'winged herald of light', and Martial wrote, 'rise for the crested birds of light resound everywhere'. Edward Thomas described two cocks crowing together as 'heralds of splendour ... cleaving the darkness

Colonel Mordaunt's Cock Match,
coloured engraving by
Richard Earlom after the painting
by Johann Zoffany, 1792.

Black swan from *The Birds of Australia*
by John Gould, 1848–69.

with a silver blow'; and for Ted Hughes the first sleepy cock crows were like 'soft rockets', gathering into a tremendous firework display; but many others would echo Charles Sedley: 'Thou cursed cock with thy perpetual noise/Mayst thou be capon made and lose thy voice/Mayst thou be punished for St Peter's crime/Thou first and worst disturber of man's rest.' St Peter's denial that he knew Jesus, which was predicted at the Last Supper – 'before the cock crows you will deny me thrice' – was a memorable symbol of a moment of weakness in the founding father of the Christian church, and for many it made the cockerel a bird of ill omen.

Many birds, including cockerels (in France), have been used as emblems by nations or individuals: the condor of Argentina, Chile, Bolivia and Colombia; the eagle of Germany and the Austrian Hapsburgs; the golden pheasant of China; and the green pheasant of Japan. In Australia, and more officially Western Australia, the emblematic bird is the black swan, a creature that was proverbial in Europe ever since the Roman writer Juvenal gave it as an example of something impossible (*rara avis*). Of course the Australian Aboriginals knew it well; it was the ancestral bird of the Nyungar people, from which they developed in the Dreamtime, and there were many stories of transformations. The first reliable European record of black swans (as distinct from earlier rumour) was that of the Dutch explorer Willem de Vlamingh, whose expedition in 1696–7 sighted black swans and named the Swan River in Western Australia after them. Captain Cook and Governor Phillip (who established the penal colony in 1789) both described them as common enough in the Botany Bay area, but by the time John Gould was in Australia (1838–40) he feared they would be hunted to extinction for 'mere wantonness'.

In medieval Europe, although swans were eaten at feasts, they were marked and protected and a number of noble families took them as their emblems, along with romantic claims to be descended from the Arthurian swan knight. In fourteenth-century England, swans were the badge of the Bohun family and when the heiress Mary married the future Henry IV they became also a Lancastrian badge. In

Swan as a livery badge from the *Sherborne Missal*, c.1399–1407.

119

St John and the eagle from the
London *Hours*, c.1407.

the *Sherborne Missal* the swan emblem appears alongside the arms of the Prince of Wales, their son, the future Henry V. This interesting mark of allegiance helps date the manuscript to around 1400, the same date as the swan livery badge found at Dunstable priory, an exquisite jewel of gold and white enamel designed to be worn by a high-ranking member of the Lancastrian camp.

Of all the worldwide stories of transformations between humans and birds, tales of swans are among the most prevalent. Legends from India and the ancient Near East hatched the idea of a swan maiden who remained with a mortal husband, but only while some taboo was unbroken. But for variations on this 'swan lake' theme, Ireland was the 'swan abounding land', and 'The Wooing of Etaine' the most compelling story. Originally married to Midir, lord of the underworld, Etaine was reborn and married Eochaid, King of Ireland. Midir won her back at last, despite all her new husband's attempts to resist his wiles and demands. He swept Etaine into his arms and they flew away as two swans linked together by golden chains around their necks. Irish poets have swan lore in their blood. Seamus Heaney evoked them tranquil on a lake – 'their feathers roughed and ruffling, white on white'; and overhead – 'the bell-beat of their wings'; and Yeats revived the ancient Greek myth of Zeus impregnating Leda in the form of a swan: 'A sudden blow; the great wings beating still/Above the staggering girl, her thighs caressed/By the dark webs, her nape caught in his bill,/He holds her helpless breast upon his breast.' Zeus also took the form of an eagle, as did many primitive sky gods before him, and his Roman equivalent Jupiter after him, making the bird a symbol of empire and battle standards, a powerful, cruel, high-soaring creature 'that', as Chaucer put it, 'with his sharp look pierces the sun'. An apotheosis was originally the ritual to deify a dead Roman emperor. As the ceremonial funeral pyre burned, a caged eagle was released to fly upward carrying the emperor's soul back to the gods. These associations with fire, immortality and the sun endowed the eagle with qualities similar to the phoenix (coming to life again as flames from the sun burned its feathers), which induced the medieval philosopher Albertus Magnus to counteract superstition with science: 'In the two eagles which I kept I observed no changes of this sort, for they moulted in the same manner as other birds of prey'.

Eagles were too good a symbol not to be absorbed into Christian tradition, although much confusion arose between the two Saints John whose emblem they became. First, the disciple and evangelist who wrote the Gospel 'In the beginning was the Word'; secondly, St John of Patmos, author of the apocalyptic Book of Revelation. It was the latter who initiated the symbols of the four Evangelists in one of his visions of a throne with these four creatures around it – including the eagle of St John. It has never been clear since whether the eagle lectern in churches, or an eagle glaring fiercely at a saint holding a pen, represents one or the other or both. Here it is St John of Patmos, gazing

towards heaven for his Revelation. The eagle is also a symbol of justice and as such appeared in Paradise in Canto 19 of Dante Alighieri's *Divine Comedy*. As Dante mounted through the spheres of the planets towards heaven he came to Jupiter. There he saw an injunction to earthly rulers to observe justice. The words then transformed into the shape of an enormous eagle incorporating the souls of those who had achieved this (the greatest were in the eye of the eagle, but this was beyond artistic powers to convey). The link with the Roman eagle was significant, because Dante believed a strong and just successor to the Roman empire would be the ideal government to end wars and factions and bring universal peace and equilibrium. Dante also suggested in this Canto that non-Christians who had led an exemplary life would be included in heaven (and in this image of the eagle), through the inscrutable workings of divine justice.

Dante and Beatrice Before the Eagle of Justice, illumination by Giovanni di Paolo from *Divina Commedia* by Dante Alighieri, c.1450.

CHAPTER SEVEN

Oddity and Humour

Humour comes in many forms, from subtle to satirical to cruel, although to be laugh-out-loud funny it needs to be surprising and immediate. But in a more mellow form it can survive over many centuries, gathering layers of significance, and recognisable through constant repetition. This was certainly the case with Aesop's *Fables*, which inaugurated that old chestnut of the birds choosing a king. In one version the doves were under attack from a kite and chose a falcon as their king, but his depredations proved even worse – a theme with resonance in any age. In this version, illustrated and updated in seventeenth-century mode by Francis Barlow, a Parliament of Birds has gathered with a peacock strutting in its centre arguing the merits of gorgeous appearance in a leader: 'And first a graceful personage should be/The prime appendix unto Majesty.' Then a magpie spoils it (like the crow in the *Fables of Pilpay*): 'Who said a king should not be gay alone/But should have courage to assert his throne.' Was this a dig at the recently restored Charles II? This edition of Aesop, the most highly regarded of Francis Barlow's works, was published in 1665. Later in his career Barlow produced far more satirical work, joining the scurrilous printmakers who opposed James II and Catholic tyranny, and his beautiful paintings of bird scenes included decoys and traps which have been interpreted as representing Popish Plots. The fashion for painting parkland filled with a variety of birds (often including the latest exotics) became very popular in seventeenth-century Europe, and in England Barlow was its leading exponent. Here his Parliament of Birds includes a frizzle fowl, turkey, ostrich and parrot.

Aesop was the first named source of animal fables, and Greek authorities, including the historian Herodotus, claimed he was a real person living in the sixth century BC, but the oral tradition of using birds and animals for exemplary and amusing tales existed everywhere and Aesop simply became the authorial name attached to the genre. Plato and Aristotle quoted him, and Aristophanes wrote whole plays in the same idiom; the Romans disseminated his fables in Latin; and in every generation foxes taunted crows, birds took revenge, and hawks caught scrawny little nightingales and refused to release them because a bird in the hand is worth two in a bush. Aristophanes' play *The Birds* was the source of Cloud Cuckoo Land, a city built in the sky by birds at the instigation of two comic Athenians tired of their city's disputes and military ventures. In 414 BC, when *The Birds* was staged, the city-state of Athens was fighting the Peloponnesian War against Sparta and had embarked on a disastrous attack on Syracuse in neutral Sicily. Athenian democracy had been established for about a hundred years, and the original bawdy plays in honour of the wine god Dionysus had accrued a wealth of contemporary satire, with barbs aimed at leading dignitaries. It can be assumed that the bird costumes and masks in Aristophanes' play were thin disguises, especially that of the moulting hoopoe who persuaded the birds to undertake the venture, and who said the life of birds was easy, just consisting of eating and adultery. To the birds, humans were 'entities without wings, insubstantial as dreams', but as Cloud Cuckoo Land was built – the woodpecker acting as carpenter and the geese shovelling mortar with their webbed feet – there were reports that in the world below people were adopting plumage.

When Chaucer wrote his long poem 'The Parliament of Fowls' around 1380, he was following this tradition of animal fable and social satire. The different orders of birds vividly represent the Lords and Commons of a medieval parliament failing to relate to one another, while the romantic dilemma they are called upon to consider is a parody of the conventions of courtly love. Each bird has a telling adjective: chattering pie (magpie); scorning jay (for its querulous screech); frosty fieldfare (the bird is a winter visitor from Scandinavia); throstle old (referring to the grizzled

OPPOSITE: 'The Parliament of Birds', illustration by Francis Barlow from *Aesop's Fables*, 1666.

The winged nation did in Councell meete
When thus the Peacock did that Iuncto greete
Saying since this day's fixt a king t' elect
We ought his full endowments to detect
And first a gracefull personage should be
The prime apendixe vnto Majestie

This being voted the bold Peacock struts
And in his clame for sovereigntie puts
Saying his Features might the crowne extort
Which vote they all but ye wise Pye support
Who sayd a king should not be gay alone
But should haue courage to assert his throne

A Prince elected should be still indu'd

Not with gay forme but inward fortitude.

F A B. XVI. *De Columbis & Accipitre.*

brown and white feathers on a thrush's breast); the false lapwing full of treachery (because it pretends to be wounded to distract attention from its nest); the waker (watchful) goose; and the eel's foe the heron. This last brings Chaucer particularly close to John Siferwas, the illuminator of the *Sherborne Missal*, who depicted two herons, one actually swallowing an eel and the other closing its beak on a trailing marginal decoration. In the Parliament, the aristocratic birds of prey believe the contest of love should be resolved by a trial of strength; the goose (representing the water fowl) says the female eagle should choose who she loves best, which the sparrowhawk dismisses as 'parfit reason for a goose'; the turtle dove (representing the birds that eat seeds) thinks all three suitors should remain true to her forever, which the duck considers pointless; the cuckoo (representing the birds that eat worms) reckons they should all remain single – which earns him a fierce snub. When the dispute has lasted till sunset all the birds make a clamorous noise: 'Have done and let us wend/When shall your cursed pleading have an end … The goos, the cokkow, and the doke also/So cryede "Kek kek! kokkow! quek quek!" hye,/That through myne eres the noyse wente tho.' But, even before Chaucer referenced bird calls that are still in use, a drollery in the *Gorleston Psalter* (a lively, rabbit-infested example of East Anglian manuscript illumination dated around 1310) showed a duck being carried off by a fox and dolefully uttering 'queck'.

Manuscript drolleries with birds often show ludicrous hunting scenes, or grotesques taking on the form of large beaked creatures shooting arrows at tiny people, or hens, ducks and geese innocently listening to foxes disguised as clerics preaching. Occasionally a drollery captures individual bird behaviour vividly. The osprey, for instance, diving with great velocity down into the water where two fish glide through the waves, appeared in an early thirteenth-century manuscript which also depicted salmon leaping. Humour, for those privileged to understand, can be intensified by a degree of obscurity. When Hamlet said (in Act 2, Scene 2) he was only mad when the wind was 'north-north-west; when the wind is southerly I know a hawk from a handsaw',

ABOVE: Duck caught by a fox from the *Gorleston Psalter*, c.1310.

OPPOSITE TOP: Geese hanging a fox from the *Smithfield Decretals*, early 14th century.

OPPOSITE LEFT: Osprey diving from *Topographia Hiberniae* by Gerald of Wales, c.1196–1223.

OPPOSITE RIGHT: Crane and fox with vase from the *Rutland Psalter*, c.1260.

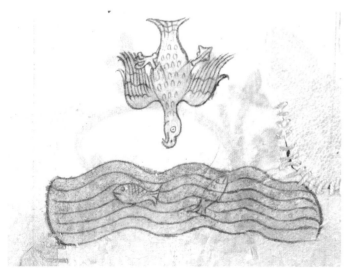

the joke is lost on those who do not know that 'hansaw' is short for heronshaw, a young heron, and Shakespeare is contrasting the flight patterns of the two birds. Humour may also be unintentional; this procession, about to be set in motion by owls, is the triumph of an academic, a scene of pride and pomp based on Roman rituals and revived in Renaissance Italy. The robed academic, from the University of Padua, sits in his chariot holding his great work, as fat little putti harness the owls and prepare to goad them into movement with sticks. Since owls are symbols of wisdom the choice is obvious, but the proposition is absurd, and they look so dubious that if the humour is unintentional it is all the better.

Thomas Bewick, the much-loved wood-engraver of the two-volume *History of British Birds* (1797–1804) introduced humour into what was a most painstaking artistic pursuit. By working on the end-grain of boxwood (often on a tiny scale) and carefully varying the depths of the engraved grooves, Bewick and those he trained developed woodblock printing from a crude medium to a very fine one, able to capture small details of a bird's plumage and jizz. In the spirit of manuscript drolleries Bewick added lively little vignettes of rural life known as tailpieces – children searching for birds' nests or building snowmen, runaway carts, or gibbets and gravestones beneath the staring owls. Bewick's illustrations did much to increase the spirit of keen observation among potential birdwatchers of his age, and his small volumes acted literally as pocket books. Naturally he included puffins (found on the rocky cliffs of Britain in great quantities), but presumably it was the recent discovery of the Falkland Islands that led him to include penguins among British birds: 'They inhabit the Southern Ocean and those desolate regions of ice and snow. The wings are properly fins being totally useless for flight though they amazingly facilitate progress through the water. The thick short feathers resemble scales in compactness and almost in texture.'

Among curious birds ostriches were favourites both in drolleries and bestiaries. Illuminators tried comically to convey their superhuman size and flightlessness, their striding legs and feet, the luxuriant eyelashes that protect

GREAT AUK.

PUFFIN.

OPPOSITE: 'Triumph of an Academic',
illumination by Franco dei Russi,
possibly from an academic diploma
of the University of Padua, c.1465–70.

ABOVE: Penguin and puffin
from *History of British Birds* by
Thomas Bewick, 1797–1804.

their enormous eyes (larger than their brains) from the sun's
glare, their desirable plumes and the long-held belief that
they digest iron – hence the drolleries of startled ostriches
with horseshoes hurtling towards them. In 1646 Thomas
Browne, author of *Pseudodoxia Epidemica*, turned his analytical
mind to this proposition with some perplexity, knowing
that many birds swallow stones for their digestion's sake. He
cited the authorities from Aristotle onwards and debated
'whether these fragments of iron swallowed by the ostrich in
some way supply the use of teeth, by commolition, grinding
and compression'. The fascination with ostriches went back
to the dawn of time; they are among the few birds to be
depicted in cave paintings, both in the Tassili caves of North

TOP: Bar Yokhnai seated on an egg from a Hebrew manuscript, 1277–86.

ABOVE: Feeding horseshoes to ostriches, from the *Queen Mary Psalter*, 1310–20.

OPPOSITE: Mr Simmons as Mother Goose in the pantomime of the same name, 1807.

Africa and the San rock art of South Africa, where the figures are part-ostrich and part-human – once again suggesting the close association of birds with shamanism. In southern Africa, ostrich dances are still performed in imitation of their impressive courtship display, in which the male flaps his wings violently and the female runs round him in circles until he winds his neck in a spiral motion.

The resulting egg, enormous and glistening, was an obvious candidate for the cosmic egg of creation mythology, and was later adopted by Islam for mosque lamps and in Christianity, from Coptic to Catholic, as a symbol of resurrection. In Piero della Francesca's Montefeltro altarpiece of the *Virgin and Child with Saints* (1472–4) it was also the emblem of the Dukes of Urbino. The magnificent egg in this Hebrew manuscript seems inspired by an ostrich, but it was laid by a mythical bird called Bar Yokani. The Old Testament had a low opinion of ostriches, claiming that they wailed in the wilderness, and they were maligned by the prophets who thought they trod on their young. But Bar Yokani was a symbol of messianic hope – although the tale attached to its egg was that it once fell from the sky and its contents swamped many cities and 300 cedar trees. In India the idea arose that the cosmic egg was golden and in Aesop's *Fables* this was transformed into the goose that laid the golden eggs. Finally the egg merged with Mother Goose (who would ride through the air on a very fine gander dispensing nonsense rhymes) to create the pantomime, first staged in the Regency period with Joseph Grimaldi, the greatest clown of all time, and recreated in 1902 for Dan Leno. In both cases the classic device of dressing a man as the leading elderly lady was employed with hilarious results, although the story went through the usual agonies of losing the source of the golden egg.

Parrots are the most obliging of all the birds that have lent themselves to human amusement. Adapting well enough to caged life, they are vividly ornamental as well as diverting, enriched with literary, seafaring and humorous allusions. The first parrot known to Europe was the green Alexandrine parrot, said to have been introduced from the

Mr SIMMONS as MOTHER GOOSE,

In the Popular new Pantomime. 1807

"*Nay doubt not, While she's kindly us'd, she'll lay*"
"*A Golden Egg on each succeeding Day.*"

—— P & E. Colour'd. ——

Punjab by Alexander the Great in 326 BC, and praised by Latin poets including Ovid: 'your beak dyed scarlet spotted with saffron ... you could dim emeralds with your fragile feathers'. Occasionally other breeds survived the medieval journey from the East. Emperor Frederick II included in his treatise on falconry several illustrations of a white and yellow cockatoo with its crest falling backwards. He said it was sent to him by the 'Sultan of Babylon', although its native place of origin was east of the Moluccas (beyond the Wallace Line). By the seventeenth century, Jan Brueghel and his contemporaries, when they painted massed wildlife in Eden, were able to depict parrots and macaws from Africa, Asia and America based on the menagerie kept by the Hapsburg Archdukes Albert and Isabella in Brussels. In paintings of Dutch interiors with girls, parrots in cages might signify virginity, and when released seduction; in still lifes their meaning was more enigmatic and in the 'Ballad of May Colven' more dramatic. She had taken revenge on her murderous abductor, false Sir John, but when her parrot asked her what had become of him she feared the outcome:

> Up then spake the pretty parrot
> 'May Colven where have you been
> What has become of false Sir John
> That went with you yestreen?'
> 'Oh hold your tongue my pretty parrot
> Nor tell no tales of me
> Your cage shall be made of the beaten gold
> And the spokes of ivory.'

OPPOSITE: May Colven and her parrot, illustration by Arthur Rackham, from *Some British Ballads*, 1919.

Edward Lear is now best remembered for his nonsense rhymes rather than his excellent illustrations of parrots, but as two sides of his wistful, self-deprecating personality they were surprisingly close. 'Verily I am an odd bird,' he wrote, sketching himself thus with other nonsense bird figures and various owl and parrot rhymes. (The 'old person in gray whose feelings were tinged with dismay' purchased two parrots and fed them on carrots.) Lear's own life was a struggle against epilepsy and ill health, aggravated by the humiliation of his poor origins and ugliness, and his own dismay and melancholy were very real: he called them 'The Morbids'. The last image he ever drew was a landscape with a small figure on a tropical island gazing out to sea, a parrot quite still in the bottom corner, and a line of flying birds escaping across the sky. Perhaps Lear loved his parrots all the more because they were trapped in the zoo.

Regent's Park Zoo opened in 1828 and Lear, only just entering his twenties, seized the initiative to produce a collection of luxury folios of these most fashionable birds, the parrots. His was the first monograph and he excelled in depicting their complex movements and quizzical expressions, and in giving their feathers a characteristic finish like scales. 'P was a Polly all red, blue and green/The most beautiful Polly that ever was seen', Lear wrote later in his nonsense alphabet. The plates were published to acclaim (but expensively) between 1830 and 1832, and the experience was a nightmare: 'I have pretty great difficulty in paying my monthly charges for printing, and the tardy paying of many of my subscribers makes it too difficult to procure food'. From then on Lear published his bird paintings in collaboration with John Gould, who worked as a taxidermist at the zoo and was inspired by Lear to take up bird illustration. Being a far stronger personality, full of energy and commercial acumen, Gould proceeded to subsume Lear's work in his own. However, for his parrot studies, Lear was recognised by the Linnean Society as 'an artist devoted to subjects of natural history', and its president Lord Stanley (after whom the Stanley parakeet was named) commissioned Lear to draw his own bird collection at Knowsley Hall

OPPOSITE: Collared parakeet from *Illustration of the family of Psittacidæ* by Edward Lear, 1832.

ABOVE: 'There was an Old Man of Dunrose; a Parrot seized hold of his Nose' from *More Nonsense* by Edward Lear, 1889.

after he became Earl of Derby in 1834. It was during Lear's visits there that he began to develop his nonsense idiom to amuse his patron's grandchildren, and perhaps as a layer of protection against his patrician sponsors. In his later years, living abroad and concentrating on landscape art, Lear recalled his early triumphs at the zoo with wistful nostalgia, although his magnificent parrot illustrations had long since given way to nonsense birds with runcible names.

The songs and cries of birds help humans to define their characters, and sometimes there really is merriment – the green woodpecker was nicknamed 'yaffle' after the chuckling noise it makes – but for laughing out loud the kookaburra is paramount. John Gould called it the great brown kingfisher or laughing jackass, and described how it would begin with a low, gurgling, good-natured sound then rise to a more hysterical note. The kookaburra greets

136

Pileated Woodpecker,
PICUS PILEATUS, Linn.

Adult Male 1. Adult Female 2. Young Males 3, 4.

Racoon Grape, Vitis æstivalis.

the dawn and at sunset can be heard again. Being a very inquisitive bird it is 'liable to pursue a party traversing the bush, though its presence is seldom detected until it emits its extraordinary gurgling, laughing note'. This, Gould freely admitted, 'causes the traveller to jump and curse and often but a few minutes elapse before it is roasting over the fire it was so lately surveying with so much curiosity'.

But for an amusing nineteenth-century man/bird interaction the prize should go to Audubon's woodpeckers. The most beautiful (and endangered) of American woodpeckers is the ivory-billed, which Audubon compared to a Van Dyke painting, but for close observation he made do with two young pileated woodpeckers, which are very similar but less hunted. He fed them on Indian corn, nuts and fruits and observed the different ways they attacked the bark of different trees. In a cage the woodpeckers were sullen and cross and their 'whole employment consisted in attempting to escape. They regularly demolished one cage every two days until finally one was constructed of oak which defeated them'. Instead they attacked their food and water troughs, and Audubon's hand, becoming ever more 'uncleanly and unsociable'. One day he entered his study to find they had escaped through a broken bar. One woodpecker instantly flew out past him into the apple tree. The other was occupied in hammering at his books. 'They must have been at liberty some hours judging by the mischief they had done. Fatigued by my pets I opened the door and the last one, hearing the voice of his brother, alighted on the same tree. They remained half an hour as if consulting together and flew off to the South.'

OPPOSITE: Pileated woodpecker
from *The Birds of America*
by John James Audubon, 1827–38.

ABOVE: Kookaburra from
The Birds of Australia by John Gould, 1848–69.

CHAPTER EIGHT

Decorative Birds

An instinctive need for decoration is shared by birds and humans. It is a way to distinguish your own kind from another, to get a mate and to make your nest good. Take the blue booby, a large marine bird of the Pacific coasts of South America (especially the Galapagos Islands), which the Spanish first nicknamed 'bobo', meaning clown, and which intrigued Charles Darwin. Their distinguishing feature is their bright blue feet and the pigment is supplied from their diet, especially oily fish, so that the youngest, fastest birds have the bluest feet and the colour fades with age or ill health. It is therefore a delightful indicator of the most genetically promising male, and female boobies are aware of this. Courtship starts with the male strutting in front of her, flaunting his bright blue feet by raising them and stretching the webs upwards and outwards. These dance steps are accompanied by tipping his beak, his tail and his wing-tips towards the sky and whistling. The female joins in (if she fancies him) and they circle round one another for as long as it takes, both displaying their blue feet. According to some accounts this fascination with blue extends to collecting scraps of blue to decorate their nests.

Off the coast of Northumberland in northern England, a little before AD 700, less colourful but very watchable marine birds were part of the inspiration for an astounding feat of book decoration. The *Lindisfarne Gospels* were created within the community of monks living on Holy Island, and according to a colophon the script and illumination were done by Eadfrith, who was Bishop of Lindisfarne from 698 until his death in 722. Estimates of the time this task would have taken range between two and ten years, and it seems most likely that Eadfrith did it before becoming bishop, possibly when he was head of the scriptorium. Writing was an honoured profession, and when it was the Word of God being written, the work had the status of a treasure. In the 670s St Wilfrid of York had given the church at Ripon 'a marvel of great beauty hitherto unheard of in our time ... the four gospels written in letters of purest gold'. Christianity had been introduced to the British Isles – via Canterbury and Ireland – during the century preceding the creation of

the *Lindisfarne Gospels*. The monastery on Holy Island was founded in 635, under the patronage of Oswald King of Northumbria, and during this time gospels formed a large proportion of the books produced. Most were smaller books for everyday use, but the *Lindisfarne Gospels* were guarded, rescued from Viking raids, moved to places of sanctuary, watched over by their patron saint, and survived mainly because they were considered the finest example of that golden age. The Lindisfarne scriptorium was a centre of excellence, producing books for other religious foundations (four examples survive at least in part). Their prestige gained an extra aura from St Cuthbert, who arrived from Ireland via Scotland (where he calmed the Loch Ness monster) and Ripon (where he founded the monastery) and took up residence first at Lindisfarne and then nearby as a hermit in the Farne Islands where he died in 687. While Eadfrith was illuminating the gospels and dedicating them to the memory of the saint, the Venerable Bede was ensuring in his *Ecclesiastical History of the English People* that knowledge of Cuthbert's life and miracles would be preserved.

These islands are still celebrated bird sanctuaries and seasonal visitors include several types of goose whose feathers are especially suitable as quill pens. St Cuthbert, like Francis of Assisi, loved birds (protecting their nesting sites from locals in search of eggs) and various bird miracles accumulated around him, while the eider duck is known locally as the cuddy duck in his honour. But of the various colonies of seabirds that could have inspired the decoration of the gospels, cormorants come the closest in form as they fly, imperious, black and sinuous, or sit on the rocks with their beaks, necks and wings proudly extended. Cormorants do also have enormous feet, although the fierce talons added by Eadfrith, adding an element of eagle to the

OPPOSITE: Carpet page of St John from the *Lindisfarne Gospels*, c.715–20.

Luke Incipit Page from the
Lindisfarne Gospels, c.715–20.

equation, cause ornithologists to deny that these decorative birds are cormorants.

The fabulous bird patterns of the *Lindisfarne Gospels* emerged from a mixed heritage. The curvilinear motifs have their ancestry in the spirals of the Celtic Iron Age, while the interwoven bands and colours are characteristic of Anglo Saxon art. But the feature that brings the complicated patterns so dramatically to life is known technically as zoomorphic interlace. These types of bird and monster heads were sprouting in many forms and places, from carved stone to jewellery, and sometimes inspiration seems to have travelled unimaginable distances. The lively twisting forms are curiously reminiscent of archaic Chinese patterns, and on certain pages Eadfrith left small deliberate imperfections, in a display of humility linked with early oriental Christianity. (This humility was later associated with Islamic art where it is explained that only Allah can achieve perfection and no artist should dare to attempt it.) On the decorated page opposite the start of St John's Gospel one bird in the top left quarter has wings striped blue and pink, while all the other birds in the design have the stripes broken into feather patterns. This is one of the four intricate pages, with a design like a luxury carpet incorporating a cross, that face the start of each Gospel. Opposite is the huge decorated initial of the first word. St Luke's Gospel starts with a Q filled with spirals evocative of Celtic shields, and some particularly serpentine birds. In the awkward space beneath the curve of the initial letter is a marvellous example of interlacing which contrives to incorporate the birds' heads, bodies and legs. The narrow margin opposite runs down into the head and paw of a cat, suggesting it has swallowed the birds in the pattern above – surely a prelude to the humour which infiltrated manuscript decoration.

To all this breathtaking intricacy was added the gift of colour. Among the egg white and ochre, the green verdigris, and red kermes (from a Mediterranean oak), there is also blue lapis lazuli all the way from Central Asia – making the arrival of artistic influences from the East less improbable. And it is worth noting that the cormorants themselves would

have been easily recognisable in any part of the world with
a coastline, including China and Japan, where there has been
a long tradition of fishing with cormorants, allowing the
tethered birds to dive under water and then choking their
catch out on to the boat's deck.

By the end of the thirteenth century, birds that were
not only recognisable (with informed guesswork), but
realistic, were beginning to decorate manuscript borders. In
1284 the *Alphonso Psalter* (see p. 144) was being prepared as a
wedding gift for the heir to the English throne, who was only
ten. The eldest son of Edward I was named after his mother's
brother King Alphonso of Castile, but the boy's premature
death opened the way for the unfortunate reign of Edward
II. It is easy to imagine that the birds were included to
delight youthful hearts, especially the large gull perched with
characteristic cheek between the royal coats of arms, and the
crane in the left-hand margin deftly catching an arrow shot
by a tiny bowman. The large woodpigeon nestling into the
top left corner, and no doubt cooing, must be a lovebird.
The other birds are in pairs: bullfinches, goldfinches and the
woodpecker facing the kingfisher. For two more centuries
birds were used to decorate manuscript borders in a way that
emphasised their jizz and variety, above all in the *Sherborne
Missal* where the largest selection grace the Easter service.
Above the scene of Christ rising from the grave angels sing
in celebration and birds echo their praise. The same motif
was repeated by the artist John Siferwas in the opening
page of the *Lovell Lectionary*, which he produced for
Salisbury Cathedral. In this instance the birds are a pheasant
and a peacock, and although they could hardly be echoing
the angel's songs (or their flight) their glorious feathers
were often an inspiration to artists seeking to portray an
angel's wings.

Cormorant from *Chorui Hiako Shiu*,
an album of coloured drawings,
Japan, 1899.

In Europe the production of luxuriantly decorated manuscripts died out during the sixteenth century due to the spread of printing, but it reached a zenith in the courts of India, Turkey and Persia where the Islamic restrictions on depicting human and natural forms were placed in abeyance as myriad brilliant miniatures were created. The works of the twelfth-century Persian poet Nizami (who composed love lyrics and drinking songs as well as epics) were a favourite for reproducing in luxury albums. In a volume commissioned by Shah Tahmasp of Persia (r. 1524–76) the pages have golden borders; here birds and flowers surround the miniature of Shirin, seated on a shaded garden seat, receiving the portrait of Khusraw with whom she promptly falls in love. One duck floats on the ornamental pool and one bird flies overhead, as if they too await their mates; but in the golden border birds abound, as they do in any perfect garden, and as artists have been sure to suggest ever since the wall paintings of Pompeii. It was this long tradition that Paul Klee meant to evoke when he painted *Bird Garden* in 1924 (see p. 149), no longer representing real appearances but the thoughts and memories that lie behind them. Whereas Shirin's garden is railed with complicated lattice work and a red chinoiserie fence, Klee's has fragmented suggestions of wall and fence. His birds defy identification but they pick their way in a most bird-like manner among the exotic leaves. Indeed all artists play with reality. In China, Japan and Korea the delights of a garden were condensed into albums of bird and flower paintings linked with brief allusive quotations from time-honoured poets (such quotations were often carved in strategic spots in the gardens themselves). Within their own conventions these paintings were intended to be as minimal, and as expressive of something wider, as Klee's paintings. Endless repetition of the bird and flower motifs in prints, fabrics and wallpapers has not diminished their decorative quality, and occasionally the jizz of an individual bird set against the rhythm of leaves or the colour of flowers retains the true quality of art.

The most compelling bird of Far Eastern decorative art is the Manchurian crane. It is depicted more often than any other because it is a symbol of immortality and therefore

OPPOSITE: Bird among camellias from *Shi zhu zhai shu hua pu*, 'Colour prints from the Ten Bamboo Studio', by Hu Zhengyan, 1633.

RIGHT: Golden oriole among leaves from *Kyomjae hwachop*, 'Album of paintings by Kyomjae', c.1900.

auspicious in any way one would wish to interpret it; although this reputation began because cranes were believed to transport the souls of the dead to the otherworld, and some of the older legends linked to cranes are distinctly eerie. For instance, an emperor ordered a crane dance to accompany the funeral of his daughter, with the whole populace to witness it, but when the youths and maidens followed the crane dancers they led them through the great bronze doors of the tomb, which were shut and sealed forever. Crane dancers are dressed in white and accompanied by a tune composed by a musician whose master had drowned. It was said that the first time it was played it caused cranes to rise from the watery grave, stretching their necks and wings and dancing. It is the size of cranes and their angular grace that makes their courtship dancing spectacular, and their movements have been imitated ritualistically not only in China, Korea and Japan but in Central Africa and among the Aborigines of Australia. In European mythology, when the Greek hero Theseus sailed with Ariadne after escaping the Cretan labyrinth, he celebrated their arrival on Naxos with a crane dance. But the symbolism of cranes in Europe branched away from immortality, and they gained instead a reputation for watchfulness. In medieval bestiaries cranes were depicted standing on one leg and holding a stone in the other. If they fell asleep while on guard the stone would fall, thus alerting the other sleeping cranes.

Peacocks, the most decorative of all birds, 'with glowing banners wide unfurled' (in the words of a Persian poet), iridescent blue-green and crown-crested, naturally became a widespread symbol of arrogance. But in the lands of their origin, the East and especially India, they too had a watchful reputation. Their loud unearthly screeches were an excellent indicator of approaching predators, and one Chinese legend ascribed an emperor's escape from pursuing enemies to the uncanny silence of a forest of peacocks, which would normally have betrayed the presence of any human hiding there. When he regained power the emperor initiated the Chinese system of decorating civil and military service with peacock feathers. Peacocks were introduced into Europe via ancient Greece, where a different version of watchfulness

OPPOSITE: Page from *Tennen hyakkaku* (Tennen's one hundred cranes) by Kaigai Tennen, Kyoto, 1900.

RIGHT: *Bird Garden,* painting by Paul Klee, 1924. Pinakothek der Moderne, Munich.

linked the bird with the goddess Hera. Zeus killed Argus, her servant with 100 eyes, who was spying on his mistress, and Hera placed Argus' eyes in the peacock's tail. Modern research has shown that the number of eyes on a peacock's tail serve to indicate to the peahen how good a mate he would be – the showier the bird and the heavier his tail the better he withstands predators, and the stronger his chicks will prove. If a peacock's tail is pruned to reduce the total, the peahen will wander off.

In medieval and Renaissance Europe the peacock was associated with alchemy, which became mired in fraudulent claims to turn base metals into gold and discover the elixir of life, but also made important advances in chemical experimentation – and much of its occult language was designed to protect hard-earned knowledge. The stages and incantations of an alchemical process were related to colour changes and also to birds: black crow, white swan, red phoenix and blue or rainbow peacock. It would seem from the miniature in a fifteenth-century treatise called *Splendor Solis* that the appearance of a peacock in the flask was auspicious. In the surrounding scene there is music and feasting, dancing and courting, and Venus rides across the sky in her chariot pulled by doves. It is very like an earthly paradise, and in Islam that was where the peacock belonged, as a symbol of the triumph of good over evil, because peacocks attack snakes.

Australia's answer to the peacock is the lyre bird, although it lacks the former's colour and is notoriously hard to see, 'inhabiting inaccessible gullies covered with creepers and vanishing as if by magic', as John Gould wrote. When the first skin arrived in Europe in 1798, the bird's name was based on a misunderstanding of how the male raises its tail in courtship. The two long slender feathers called lyrates, in the centre of the plume, in fact fan out sideways and the filaments between them are fluffed out like a ballerina's skirt, which the bird then tips forward over its head, making the display more dramatic and daunting than the statuesque pose envisaged. The bird creates an earthen mound as a stage on which to perform, and this John Gould did see: 'here the bird

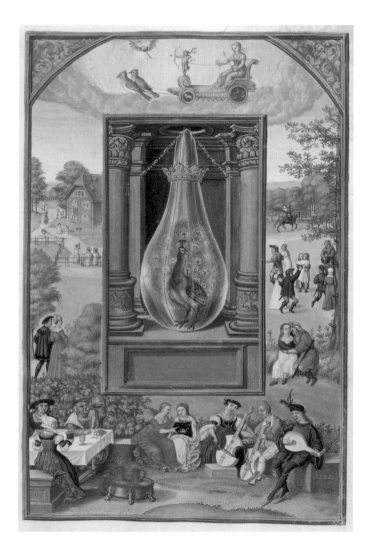

ABOVE: Peacock in a flask from *Splendor Solis*, Germany, 1582.

OPPOSITE: Lyre bird from *The Birds of Australia* by John Gould, 1848–69.

MENURA SUPERBA, *Shaw*

CHLAMYDERA MACULATA, Gould.

constantly tramples, at the same time erecting and spreading its tail in the most graceful manner and uttering various cries, either natural notes or mocking other birds and even the howling dingo'.

While for many birds their decorative feathers serve to fascinate a mate, the adornment of a nest is an alternative ploy. Birds of various species go in for delicate weaving, moulding and lining, or use value-added plant materials, cobwebs or glittering objects. The bowerbirds of Australia and New Guinea outdo them all in their obsessive collecting of decorative objects, and the structure they decorate is not a nest but a seduction parlour or, as David Attenborough put it, an art gallery. Bowerbirds inhabit the rainforest and bear a distant relationship to birds of paradise. Some have gorgeous plumage and they all perform courtship dances, but most look more like crows. It is the males that build the bowers, some of which are like tents, but most are like tunnels. At the entrance the objects of enticement are arranged. The Vogelkop bowerbird of New Guinea heaps red/orange flowers alongside dark wing-cases of beetles, or deer dung. The satin bowerbird of Australia has a stronger penchant for blue, adapted according to environment so that nowadays a pathway of blue drinking straws may lead to the entrance where deeper blue bottle tops await the inquiring female, who in the past would have hopped to her destiny over blue berries, feathers and beetle wings. The display is arranged with a sense of perspective, larger to smaller objects, which holds the attention of the female for longer – and males creating the strongest optical illusions have the highest mating success.

This behaviour may have evolved to protect the females, who in species that do not build bowers are subjected to violent sexual advances, sometimes in mid-air. The habit of bower-building ensures that the male awaits the female and only when she enters the portals is she jumped upon. If John Gould realised it was all to do with proper sexual conduct, he did not explain this to his Victorian subscribers, because he described the bowers as assembly points. But he was certainly entranced with the scale and variety of the collections. Of the satin bowerbird he wrote 'their propensity to pick up small decorative objects is so well known that the natives look there for missing items'. But it was the bleached skulls and shells assembled by the spotted bowerbird that most amazed him:

> The bower is beautifully lined with tall grasses so disposed that their heads nearly meet. Indications of design are manifest through the whole bower ... at the mouth of the run the stones form little paths while the bones, crania of small mammals and bivalve shells are placed in heaps before the entrance. Sometimes the bowers are far from the rivers from which the shells and pebbles come, and the birds have collected only objects bleached white in the sun or roasted by the natives, even seed stones have to be bleached.

In their appreciation of form and colour, and in constructing their nests or displays from selected materials, often with great effort and intricacy, birds may parallel the urges behind human decoration and art.

OPPOSITE: Spotted bowerbird from *The Birds of Australia* by John Gould, 1848–69.

Fatal Fascination

Of all the birds, from the great auk to passenger pigeons, whose extinction has been a cause of regret and warning, dodos have most captured the imagination. Their island of Mauritius was first visited by the Portuguese as they crossed the Indian Ocean, but they left no word of the dodo, and it was the Dutch who took possession in 1598, naming it after their Stadtholder Maurice of Nassau. The account of Admiral van Neck's expedition, published in 1601, included a map of the harbour – in which D marked the spot where the dodos were found – and a sketch of an athletic-looking dodo hurrying away. 'They were as big as large turkies covered with down having little hanging wings like short sleeves altogether useless to fly with,' wrote the Cornish traveller Peter Mundy in 1638; but subsequent portrayals of a fat bird on stumpy legs were misleading, either based on menagerie specimens surviving on the wrong diet, or badly stuffed skins. In Mauritius dodos probably ate fallen fruit, nuts and roots, gorging in times of plenty in preparation for seasonal scarcity, which would account for the greed mentioned by observers.

The artist mainly responsible for the image of the dodo was Roelant Savery, who initiated the seventeenth-century fashion for landscape paintings with exotic birds and beasts. His first painting to include a dodo, done in 1611 when he was working in Prague for the Hapsburg Emperor Rudolph II, was of Orpheus playing to the animals, which showed a whitish dodo. Presumably this was based on the specimen later recorded as a stuffed bird in Rudolph's collection. The only description of a dodo alive in Europe came from Hamon L'Estrange who, attracted by an advertising banner, saw one on display in London in 1638 (was this the dodo in John Tradescant's collection which passed to the Ashmolean Museum in Oxford?). Probably dodos did arrive as living birds to be kept in menageries, and were then stuffed when they died. All that now remains (in England and Denmark) are a couple of skulls and feet, and a beak in Prague, but the evidence is augmented by bones excavated in Mauritius which suggest the dodo was a coastal bird, and already localised when the Europeans arrived. Within a century they were extinct. Peter Mundy, who visited Mauritius in 1634 and 1638, failed to see dodos there although he saw one brought to Surat for the Mughal menagerie. It led him to speculate, 200 years before Darwin, 'how they should be in Mauritius and not elsewhere ... being so far from other land and can neither fly nor swim. Whether by mixture of kinds producing strange and monstrous forms, or the nature of the climate, air and earth altering the first shapes over long time'.

Roelant Savery's later paintings, done after his return to Holland in 1616, and the copy in Oxford made by his nephew Jan Savery in 1651 (which inspired Lewis Carroll to include a dodo in *Alice in Wonderland*) showed dodos as grey birds. One version came into the collection of Hans Sloane and then George Edwards (author of the *Natural History of Uncommon Birds*) who presented it to the British Museum in 1759 with the tradition that it was 'painted in Holland from the living bird' – presumably in the menagerie of Maurice of Nassau (d. 1625). Another of Savery's paintings depicted the dodo from behind with curly tail feathers, standing on one leg and turning its astonishing beak to preen its foot. Since many Dutch paintings contained proverbs and puns this may have been a play on the origins of its name, *dodaars,* which in Dutch means 'fat arse'. Savery's last and loveliest *Landscape with Birds*, painted in 1628, showed the dodo sporting a yellow tail, wing tufts and feet, standing between a cassowary and a stork (see p. 156). Far above them the golden plumes of birds of paradise drift legless across the sky. It was meant as an idyll but its unnatural plenitude was based on capture and destruction, just as the ornithologies of Gould and Audubon and the theories of Darwin and Wallace all testified to myriad birds sacrificed in the causes of scientific discovery.

Anatomically dodos were closely related to pigeons, although the stunted wings and hefty beak disguised this fact until recently. Fate decreed that another famously extinct bird should be the passenger pigeon of North America. They were distinguished by their long tails and a wine-dark blush on the breast of the male. Unlike dodos they were superabundant. As they roamed in search of seasonal nuts their passage turned day to night, their droppings fell like rain and Audubon said the noise of their wing-beats resembled a gale at sea

blowing through the rigging. Among settlers and Indians they fell victim to orgies of hunting, trading and eating until this seemingly endless resource dwindled and died out completely. The present predicament of the European turtle dove, migrating over the hunters of southern Europe, echoes the same warning – and this one family of universally familiar birds can act as a symbol for all species. The extent of the doom depends on everyone. It is reminiscent of Noah's Ark, where there was indeed a scene of devastation but the legendary dove did emerge alive.

OVERLEAF: *Landscape with Birds*, painting by Roelant Savery, 1628. Kunsthistorisches Museum, Vienna.

FURTHER READING

Simon Armitage and Tim Dee (eds),
The Poetry of Birds
(London: Penguin, 2011)

Simon Barnes,
A Bad Birdwatcher's Companion
(London: Short Books, 2005)

Caroline Bugler,
The Bird in Art
(London: Merrell, 2012)

Mark Cocker and David Tipling,
Birds and People
(London: Cape, 2013)

Wilma George,
Animals and Maps
(Berkeley, CA: University of California
Press, 1969)

Graeme Gibson,
The Bedside Book of Birds
(London: Bloomsbury, 2005)

Peter Tate,
Flights of Fancy
(London: Random House, 2007)

William Brunsdon Yapp,
Birds in Medieval Manuscripts
(London: British Library, 1981)

CAPTIONS TO PRELIMS AND CHAPTER OPENERS

Page 1: Detail of barn swallow from *The Birds of America* by John James Audubon, 1827–38.

Page 2: Detail from a version of the *Kalila va Dimna* fables, India, 1610–11.

Page 6: Detail of *Paradisea minor* from *A Monograph of the Paradiseidae; or, Birds of Paradise*, by Daniel Giraud Elliot, London, 1783.

Page 24: Spotted kingfisher from *Oriental Memoirs* by James Forbes, 1813.

Page 46: Lesser kestrel, watercolour, south India, 1793–1813.

Page 64: Detail of great northern diver from *The Birds of America* by John James Audubon, 1827–38.

Page 86: Detail from 'The Raven of ill-omen', illustration by Stephen Reid from *Cuchulain, the Hound of Ulster* by Eleanor Hull, 1909.

Page 102: Detail from Cockerel from *Chorui Hiako Shiu*, an album of coloured drawings, Japan, c.1860–70.

Page 122: 'There was an Old Man with an Owl', from *Book of Nonsense* by Edward Lear, 1885.

Page 138: Peacock from a *Book of Hours*, France, mid-15th century.

PICTURE CREDITS

All images the British Library unless otherwise stated.
Pages 94 & 156–7 Photo akg-images/Erich Lessing;
page 149 photo akg-images.

INDEX